Into Your Hands

Exploring the Seven Last Words from the Cross

Copyright © 2019 David Mercadante All rights reserved

No part of this book may be reproduced, stored in a retrieval system, or transmitted in any form, or by any means whether by electronic, mechanical, photocopy, recording or otherwise, without the prior written permission of the copyright owner except in the case of a brief quotation embodied in a critical review and certain other noncommercial uses permitted by copyright law. For all other uses, requests for permission may be sent to the publisher, "Attention: Permissions Coordinator," at the address below:

3673 Hoover Hill Rd. Sophia, NC 27370

All scripture quotations, unless otherwise indicated, are taken from the Holy Bible, New International Version ®, NIV ®. Copyright © 1973, 1978, 1984, 2011 by Biblica, Inc.™ Used by permission of Zondervan. All rights reserved worldwide. www.zondervan.com. The "NIV" and "New International Version" are trademarks registered in the United States Patent and Trademark office by Biblica, Inc.™

Scripture quotations marked (ESV) are from the Holy Bible, English Standard Version ® (ESV ®), copyright 2001 by Crossway, a publishing ministry of Good News Publishers. Used by permission. All rights reserved.

Cover art used with permission from Wall Art By Design ©

To Emily

Ecclesiastes 4:12

Table of Contents

Acknowledgements	.vi
Foreword	.vii
Introduction	1
Step One - Receiving Forgiveness	13
Father, forgive them, for they do not know what they are doing. Luke 23:34	
Step Two - New Citizenship	28
Truly I tell you, today you will be with me in Paradise. Luke 23:43	
Step Three - A New Community	44
Woman, here is your son. Here is your mother. John 19:26–27	
Step Four - Wrestling with God	58
My God, my God, why have you forsaken me? Mark 15:34; Matthew 27:46	
Step Five - New Thirst	73
I am thirsty. John 19:28	
Step Six - Confidence in Salvation	88
It is finished. John 19:30	
Step Seven - Rest in God	102
Father, into your hands I commit my spirit. Luke 23:46	
Epilogue	116
Bibliography	119
Vita	121

Acknowledgements

My prayer is that this work would give glory and honor to God. I pray this little book would encourage his church to grow into an ever-deepening relationship with Him. I have tried to write with sincere humility, knowing that the teachings of Jesus, especially from the Cross, are extraordinarily profound. There is not a single, definitive interpretation of the words from the Cross. Their depth and beauty are beyond mere words. Yet I believe that God uses these scriptures to speak to our heart. By leaning into the Seven Last Words from the Cross, we can encounter God and, in humility, learn His desire for our life. Anything worthwhile in these pages is a gift from God. If anything is clumsy or incorrect, that's all me.

This book is the culmination of hours of study and reflection on the seven last words of Jesus. It has been a joy to pour over these scriptures and explore these sayings. I hope the reader will learn something new and, most importantly, grow closer to God through His word. A special thanks to everyone who helped this project come to life. My mom, Margaret Hildreth called and texted nearly every day, anxious to read and edit the next chapters.

Another reader and friend, Christian Herring, was a constant source of encouragement. Paula Allen and Linda Justice gave helpful feedback throughout. And, of course, my best friend (and wife!), Emily, who would put down everything she was doing to read each chapter and offered important corrections and clarifications. God has blessed me with good, honest and faithful people to help me through this journey.

I am forever grateful.

Foreword

In evangelical Christianity the crucifixion of Jesus Christ rightly stands as the centerpiece of our theology and doctrine. It has been observed that the cross is the epicenter of human history, with all previous events looking forward to it, and all subsequent events somehow effected by the ripples – nay shockwaves – that reverberated out from it. The impact of the death and resurrection of Jesus cannot be overstated for either the believer or the non-believer. Whether we like it or not the course of history was changed nearly two-thousand years ago in a backwater province of the Roman Empire by a carpenter's son from Nazareth.

It would be easy to become fixated on the crucifixion event itself and get lost in the discussions about what actually happened that day at Calvary. Was Christ's death substitutionary? Was he a ransom? Was he simply an example of a life well lived that should be emulated? On and on goes the list. However, we must remind ourselves that Jesus was a person. Yes, he was God incarnate. Fully God and fully man, as mysterious and contradictory as that may sound. But let us remember that a human being died that day. A human being that had friends. A son who had an earthly step-father and a mother who loved him and watched him die the most horrific death the Romans, who were very adept at such things, could think up. He was one of us, but then again, he wasn't. He died the death that we should die, and he was the only person ever to have lived that did not deserve it. If ever there was a person worth listening to it is this man, Jesus the Christ.

For many pastors and lay people alike it is easy to make a bee-line for "it is finished" and celebrate the completion of Jesus' mission and redemption and the fulfillment of the Law. It shouldn't be shocking in a culture that is so addicted to results, instant gratification, and "what's in it for me," that we would rush to the part where our sins are forgiven and put away forever. I fear, though, that we may be missing something if we don't slow down and take the time to consider all that Jesus has to offer us from the cross. As you will see in the pages you are about to read there is much that our Savior said in his dying moments that can, and should, change our lives. If you believe, like I do, that God inspired the very words of Scripture then there is not an idle syllable in the words that flowed from Jesus' swollen, parched, and cracked lips as he hung there for you and me.

As Dave points out, we humans tend to put a high premium on last words. We want them to be meaningful so that they will be remembered and pondered for generations to come. Needless to say, the most important man in history had some very powerful last words. Through these pages you will be invited to stop and listen, absorb, hear afresh what our Great High Priest had to say as he died. Do not be discouraged, however, because even though these were Jesus' last words before he died, we must never forget that his words were words of life.

As someone who preaches and teaches on a weekly basis it has been refreshing to see another perspective on the last words of Christ, to hear how God is speaking through his Word to another one of his children. I am confident that your time spent with this book in partnership with God's Word will be a blessing. There will be moments, I pray, when you are brought to your knees in humble repentance before a just, and merciful King. On the other hand, I am confident that you will be overjoyed as you are reminded of the Good News that redemption has been secured and those who repent and believe are invited to be citizens of God's Kingdom, his forever family.

Again, as you read these pages and come in contact with the last words of Christ, I pray that you will slow down and feel the weight of the words. Hear what the Lord Jesus is saying to you. Soak in the magnificent wonder of a God who became man and loved you enough to die for you. Savor each word that was spoken for your good and God's glory.

Finally, I want to commend my dear friend Dave to you. We spent time in the trenches of seminary together. We have shared times of joy, frustration, pain, and victory, in vocational ministry, along with one or two burritos and a multitude of laughs. His dedication to the people of God, and his commitment to rightly dividing the word of truth are exemplary. As you read these pages know that they are born in a heart of love for Jesus, and for the people he came to save.

Christian R. Herring
M.Div., Th.M
Albemarle, NC

x

Introduction

Dr. V. Raymond Edman, chancellor of Wheaton College, was addressing the gathered student body in 1967. The former missionary had forged relationships with leaders all over the world, including President Nixon, Madame Chiang Kai-shek, and His Majesty Haile Selassie of Ethiopia. During the message, Edman spoke to the students about his meeting with King Haile Selassie. The Ethiopian king was worshiped by many in his home country.

Dr. Edman told the students about the strict instructions concerning decorum in the presence of the African king. He was made to memorize proper protocol that had to be followed precisely, including how to greet, when to shake hands, and what to wear. Dr. Edman told his students that the Ethiopian delegation went so far as to require a written test to make sure he knew the customs, lest he offend the king.

In the crescendo of his chapel message, Dr. Edman told the college students that they serve a different king. The only requirement to enter his presence is humility and acceptance:

> *But I speak primarily of another King. This chapel is the house of the King. Chapel is designed to be a meeting on your part with the King of kings and the Lord of lords Himself. To that end, chapel is designed for the purpose of worship... not a lecture, not an entertainment, but a time of meeting the King. Come in, sit down and wait in silence before the Lord. In so doing, you will prepare your own hearts to hear the Lord, to meet with the King. Your heart will learn to cultivate what the Scripture says, 'Be still and know that I am God.' Over these years I have learned the immense value of that deep, inner silence as David, the king, sat in God's presence to hear from him.*

Dr. Edman then took a step back from the pulpit, grabbed his chest and collapsed on the stage. He literally dropped dead. Those were the chancellor's last words. His last breath was an articulate and beautiful testimony about the God that he would meet in the next instant.[1]

Last Words

The idea of "famous last words" as a concept that captivates the human psyche. We intuitively desire to know the thoughts of a person as they pass from this life to the next. Fulton Sheen said it well: "Man's heart is always anxious to hear the state of mind of anyone at that very common, yet very mysterious moment called death."[2] Ideally, everyone would have the opportunity to craft well-articulated phrases that would summarize their lives, and there would be people around to hear the last words.

Some have expressed their final sentiments with elegant prose:

> American patriot Nathan Hale: "I only regret that I have but one life to give for my country."
>
> Poet Emily Dickinson: "I must go in; the fog is rising."
>
> Missionary William Carey: "When I am gone, speak less of Dr. Carey and more of Dr. Carey's Savior."[3]

As a pastor, I have sat at many a bedside during final hours. It is a privileged encounter, to witness the final moments of life on earth. But I'd be lying if I said most last moments were dignified, with poetic statements from the one passing. My grandfather passed away after a long, painful bout with cancer. He was a pastor for five decades and could expound on the Scriptures with fine articulation. Papa was a big man, too; he played college football when they still wore leather helmets. But at the end, his body and mind were reduced by sickness. His last words were uncomfortable, indiscernible mutters. Hardly fitting last words for such a full life. That end-of-life scene is, unfortunately, the rule rather than the exception.

Much is known about the life and ministry of Jesus. His sermons and sayings were recorded for posterity. It is a gift of insurmountable value that we get to hear his final words as well.

The last words of Jesus are precious because they tell us his final thoughts before death. Only three other people in Scripture had their last words recorded: Isaac, Moses, and Stephen. Each serves as a pivotal figure in God's revelatory history. Isaac was the first Israelite, the first in a line of chosen people. Moses had the Law revealed to him on Sinai, which would serve to bind the Hebrew people as God's chosen. Stephen was among the first Christians and was martyred for his faith. He represents the seeds of the early church that had to be broken in order to flourish.

But it is the last words of Jesus that carry the most weight. He did not offer one statement to summarize his life. Rather, there are seven statements, each delving into the heart of God and his desire for the world. As we will see, each phrase is rich with historical, theological, and personal application. The Seven Last Words are not mumbled gasps from a dying, disheartened, and misunderstood rabbi. They are a glimpse into the mind and heart of the Savior.

About the Seven Last Words

The Seven Last Words are actually seven statements of Jesus from the cross:

1. "Father, forgive them, for they do not know what they are doing" (Luke 23:34).
2. "Truly I tell you, today you will be with me in Paradise" (Luke 23:43).
3. "Woman, here is your son. . . . Here is your mother" (John 19:26–27).
4. "My God, my God, why have you forsaken me?" (Mark 15:34; Matthew 27:46).
5. "Father, into your hands I commit my spirit" (Luke 23:46).
6. "I am thirsty" (John 19:28).
7. "It is finished" (John 19:30).

Three of the statements are recorded by Luke and three others by John. The remaining word is recorded by Matthew and Mark. The diversity of recollection tells us that the gospel writers wanted to emphasize certain sayings because they were important to their specific faith communities. The gospel writers were writing to different congregations, each with certain peculiarities. For instance, John wrote to a Greek audience, Mark to a congregation of Christians who had converted from Judaism. The diversity of recollection among the gospel writers is a glimpse into the perspective of the early church and what they valued in their respective congregations. Jesus may have uttered more words from the cross, but those that are recorded are a reflection of the specific context for each gospel writer.

Each word was spoken to a certain audience and in a context that will be discussed in each chapter. The historical order in which they were spoken is up for debate because differing recollections of the gospel writers. As early as the second century, the church began to order the Seven Last Words for liturgical purposes, to help Christians meditate on these sayings.[4] That there are seven sayings is often perceived as divine providence. The number seven is a symbol of completion, a fact not lost on mystics through the ages.

By the sixteenth century, the Seven Last Words were commonly used in worship, especially in the Lenten season. Franz Joseph Haydn famously created an orchestral ensemble about the Seven Last Words, prompting modern authors to write devotional pieces about the music! Christians of all stripes use the Seven Last Words in Good Friday worship, often with a three-hour (or longer) service of prayers, recitations, and music on each statement. The Seven Last Words have been pondered over and mulled perhaps more than other phrases in Christian history. As we journey through these Seven Last Words, we will join millennia of believers who have meditated upon these beautiful phrases.

Jesus and His Pulpits

As we begin, we must consider: do we want to hear a message from the cross?

Jesus taught and preached in a lot of different places. He used a pulpit in Nazareth and proclaimed himself the Messiah. People enjoyed that message until he said the gospel would go to the entire world. Then they tried to throw him off a cliff.[5] But not every crowd was so hostile. The masses were getting restless and hungry as Jesus taught in the wilderness. Rejecting the disciples' request to send them away, Jesus turned a small portion of bread and fish into enough to feed the thousands.[6] Those crowds enjoyed Jesus's message.

On another occasion, he preached from the mountainside and offered words of insight and consolation that are quoted by believers and non-believers alike: "love your enemies" and "judge not, lest you be judged." Bits and pieces of the Sermon on the Mount have become common nomenclature, even in secular society.[7]

Jesus's sermon from the Mount of Olives in Matthew 23- 25 has a sharper tone. Overlooking Jerusalem, Jesus acted as a firebrand, calling down doom and "woe" on the hypocrites inside the great city. Some resonate with this type of firebrand sermon, which calls out spiritual hypocrisy.

Jesus preached or taught from a boat, a living room, a crowd, a healing pool, and on the shore, just to name a few places. He taught at a well[8] and a mountaintop[9]; Jesus preached the truth of God. And listeners, even detractors, were anxious to hear his message. Except from the cross.

Very few people were able to embrace his message from the cross. Almost all of his disciples fled, with only five faithful witnesses remaining to see the crucifixion. The others around the cross either embraced his last words as divine, mocked him, or brushed his words off as the meanderings of a failed revolutionary.

The Cross Makes for a Reluctant Audience

In my experience, few want to grapple with the preaching of Jesus from the cross. We will listen to him as he strolls along Galilee, preaching a message of love and peace. We will listen after the resurrection, enjoying the victory over death. But what about the pulpit of the cross? There are a few reasons we do not like to listen to the crucified Preacher.

First, the cross causes us to witness the scope of human brutality. At Calvary, we see the worst of us. To crucify a criminal is less about justice and more about humiliation. The idea is to inflict as much pain on the convicted as possible. Naked, impaled, and shamed for all the world to see: the cross is an emblem of how awful we can be to one another.

"But I would never do that to another person!" we like to tell ourselves. Perhaps we would avoid the bloody deed, but who among us can deny the sins that led Jesus to his judgment day? The crucifixion is the culmination of resentments, gossip, lies, and deceit. You without sin can cast the first stone.

The cross is the bloody result of the seeds of scorn sown against our Savior. Throughout his ministry, there were enemies who accused him of everything from blasphemy to gluttony. Those baseless accusations could have been leveled by any one of us. We are all sinful and guilty. The empty cross has (rightly) become a symbol of victory over death, hung in sanctuaries and casually worn as jewelry. But when Jesus occupied the cross, he was an "emblem of suffering and shame."[10] Would we want to hear someone speak from their misery? Especially if our sin was complicit in driving the nails and creating the agony? Give us the megachurch lectern or the traditional oak pulpit, but not a message from the bleeding Savior, lest we are reminded of our complicity in the cross.

A second reason we may ignore the pulpit of the cross is it reminds us of the suffering required to follow Jesus. The word "Christian" means "little Christ." To call yourself a Christian means more than the acceptance of doctrine. Faith in Christ is more than "fire insurance" from the depths of hell. To receive Jesus as Savior means we devote our lives to his teachings and submit ourselves to his Way. This, as Jesus explains to his followers, inevitably requires suffering.

Jesus warned his followers before accepting the call to discipleship:

> *'If anyone comes to me and does not hate father and mother, wife and children, brothers and sisters—yes, even their own life—such a person cannot be my disciple. And whoever does not carry their cross and follow me cannot be my disciple.*
>
> *'Suppose one of you wants to build a tower. Won't you first sit down and estimate the cost to see if you have*

> *enough money to complete it? For if you lay the foundation and are not able to finish it, everyone who sees it will ridicule you, saying, "This person began to build and wasn't able to finish."*
>
> *'Or suppose a king is about to go to war against another king. Won't he first sit down and consider whether he is able with ten thousand men to oppose the one coming against him with twenty thousand? If he is not able, he will send a delegation while the other is still a long way off and will ask for terms of peace. In the same way, those of you who do not give up everything you have cannot be my disciples.'*[11]

The message is clear: Following Jesus requires sacrifice. The Way is a path of suffering. The disciple may be called to sell everything and give the money to the poor.[12] Sure, you are blessed, but only when you hunger, mourn, and undergo persecution.[13] The Christian has a tall order: to reject sin and aim for the perfection of Jesus,[14] while loving sinners and defending them against religious zealots. It ain't easy.

In my experience, few are willing to accept the Way of Jesus. Hordes of curious seekers grace Sunday morning services looking for a composite of entertainment and spiritual satisfaction. They will enjoy a worship service and may jump into a community activity. But suffering? No thanks.

It reminds me of an old story of a pilgrim traveling to the Holy Land in the Middle Ages. The devoted soul was on a pilgrimage to Jerusalem and carrying a large cross as a way to imitate Jesus on the way to Calvary. As he got closer to his destination, the cross became increasingly heavy with each step. He trudged on under the increasingly heavy weight until he reached a small town outside the city. While resting, he reluctantly asked a carpenter to cut a few feet off of the cross to lighten the load. The carpenter complied and sawed off a large portion of the bottom of the cross. The cross, now lighter, was easier to carry. Just before entering the Holy Land, the pilgrim came across a gully and needed a bridge to get across. The cross, now trimmed and lighter, was too short to bridge the divide. The pilgrim turned around and went home, never reaching his destination.[15]

That story is piercing. Suffering is part and parcel of the Christian experience. It is a weight to bear. Of course, we do not believe in salvation by works or that suffering is necessarily a means of grace. But to diminish the suffering of the Way of Christ is to neglect a key aspect of our calling as "little Christs." While many Christians clamor for the glory of a worship experience, just to be close to him or "sit at his right hand" as the disciples wanted, John the Baptist reminds us that Jesus does not baptize with cool, fresh water, but with consuming fire.[16]

A third reason we may avoid the pulpit of the cross is we must face a mortal Savior. On Calvary, Jesus was in the fullness of his humanity. Through the centuries, Christians have grappled with the theological implications of God in human flesh. Jesus is God, in all his resplendent power and majesty. God is Jesus, in all his frail, tattered flesh. This is a mystery not to be solved, but leaned into. The cross forces us to consider the unique aspect of our Christian faith: that God became incarnate in the person of Jesus Christ.

God became his creation in order to empathize and therefore save his fallen children. "For God so loved the world that He sent His only begotten son, that whosoever would believe in Him would not perish, but have everlasting life."[17]

Paul dances with this theological notion in his first letter to the Corinthians: "God made him who had no sin to be sin for us, so that in him we might become the righteousness of God."[18]

The writer of Hebrews reminds us that God commiserates with us: "For we do not have a high priest who is unable to empathize with our weaknesses, but we have one who has been tempted in every way, just as we are—yet he did not sin."[19]

In hearing the Seven Last Words, we acknowledge that Jesus is fully human. He is one of us. He knew pain and temptation, betrayal and suffering. At the cross, we cannot pretend that Jesus was just a divine being or simply a good, moral teacher. At Calvary, we meet Jesus who is one with God and one with us. The

Incarnate Savior. This profound truth reminds us that Jesus is close to us. He has entered our human condition. He has come to where we live. This is not some distant watch-maker god who set creation in motion and leaves it to its own devices. Rather, Jesus has carried our flesh, suffered our pains, and cried our tears.

The Seven Last Words and Spiritual Progression

The cross is a bloody reminder of our brutality and mortality. But, if we are bold enough to approach Calvary's preacher, there is an invitation to a rich and full experience with Jesus. The Seven Last Words can be a guide to an ever-deepening life with God. Christian maturity does not happen in an instant. It is a lifelong process that requires our consistent response to the prompting of the Holy Spirit. In his ministry, Jesus called his disciples to a progressively deeper life with him:

"Come, follow me."[20]
"Come to me."[21]
"Come and see."[22]
"Go and tell."[23]

On this side of heaven, there is no "final destination" in our life with Christ. There is always room to grow. Christians have a long history of articulating the various stages of spiritual growth. While it is impossible to fully explain an ever-deepening spiritual life, some have pieced together stages of spiritual growth using analogies and images.

The apostle Paul described the difference between spiritual immaturity and maturity using food as an analogy.

> *Brothers and sisters, I could not address you as people who live by the Spirit but as people who are still worldly mere infants in Christ. I gave you milk, not solid food, for you were not yet ready for it. Indeed, you are still not ready.*[24]

A couple of centuries later, Origen of Alexandria likened the forty-two encampments of the Hebrew people (found in Numbers

33) to individual stages of spiritual growth. Each of the encampments is comparable to another stage of spiritual progression toward peace with God.

Teresa of Avila described the deep life with God as a castle with separate "dwelling places." In her classic work *The Interior Castle*, Teresa described the movement of the soul from room to room, each one representing a deeper relationship with God. Through spiritual discipline and devotion, the believer takes steps toward intimacy with God, eventually reaching the inner "mansion."[25]

John Wesley was even more linear in his understanding of spiritual maturity. Christians could progress in noticeable stages, eventually reaching "entire sanctification."

As we journey through the Seven Last Words of Jesus together, I would like to consider them as a pathway to spiritual maturity, with each word representing an opportunity to step closer to a deeper life with God.

> Step One - **Receiving Forgiveness.** "Father, forgive them, for they do not know what they are doing" (Luke 23:34).
>
> Step Two - **New Citizenship.** "Truly I tell you, today you will be with me in Paradise" (Luke 23:43).
>
> Step Three - **A New Community.** "Woman, here is your son. Here is your mother" (John 19:26–27).
>
> Step Four- **Wrestling with God.** "My God, my God, why have you forsaken me?" (Mark 15:34; Matthew 27:46).
>
> Step Five - **New Thirst.** "I am thirsty" (John 19:28).
>
> Step Six - **Confidence in Salvation.** "It is finished" (John 19:30).
>
> Step Seven - **Rest in God.** "Father, into your hands I commit my spirit" (Luke 23:46).

If we dare to approach the pulpit of the cross, we are starting a journey to the heart of Christ. It is hard to listen to the words of a suffering man. But these words, though uttered in the throes of pain, express the heart of our Savior and offer a pathway to divine rest.

---

[1] Joel S. Woodruff, "Profile in Faith: V. Raymond Edman: President of Wheaton College, Mentor to Billy Graham." C.S. Lewis Institute. Winter 2011. http://www.cslewisinstitute.org/Profile_In_Faith_V_Raymond_Edman_ SinglePage.

[2] Fulton Sheen, *Life of Christ* (New York: Double Day Publishing, 1990), 122.

[3] Steven Furtick, *Seven-Mile Miracle: Experience the Last Words of Christ As Never Before*. (Colorado Springs, CO: Multnomah Press, 2017). 11.

[4] James Martin. *Seven Last Words: An Invitation to a Deeper Friendship with Jesus*. Kindle Edition. (New York: HarperOne, 2015), 7.

[5] Luke 4:28-30

[6] Matthew 14:13-21

[7] Matthew 5-7

[8] John 4:1-26

[9] Matthew 17:1-11

[10] From the hymn, "Old Rugged Cross" by George Bennard, 1915, verse 1.

[11] Luke 14:26-33

[12] Matthew 19:16-30

[13] Matthew 5:3-12

[14] Matthew 5:48

[15] Erwin W. Lutzer, *Cries from the Cross: A Journey into the Heart of Jesus* (Chicago: Moody Publishers, 2015), Kindle Edition. 8-9

[16] Matthew 3:11

[17] John 3:16

[18] 1 Corinthians 5:21

[19] Hebrews 4:15

[20] Matthew 4:19

[21] Matthew 11:28

[22] John 1:39-41

[23] March 16:15

[24] 1 Corinthians 3:1-2

[25] Teresa of Avila. *Interior Castle*. (New York, N.Y.: Doubleday, 1988)

Step One - Receiving Forgiveness

"Father, forgive them, for they do not know what they are doing." Luke 23:34

The first step in a relationship with God is the acceptance of God's forgiveness through the shed blood of Jesus Christ. By his atoning death, our sins are covered and we can commune with God. Without that covering, there is condemnation. Many believe that being "good" will cover their sins. But no amount of good deeds, church attendance, charity, or religious observance can cover our sin. Only the shed blood of Jesus can cover our offenses before God.

The only reason we can be in relationship with God is because he is good and forgiving. This marks an important distinction in the Christian faith: we cannot earn our way to God. John put it succinctly: "We love God because God first loved us."[1]

His love is the originator of our faith. In seeking a relationship with God, we must first receive the forgiveness he offers through his Son. To seek God without first receiving his forgiveness is a fruitless exercise. It is like trying to swim without getting wet. So we begin with *Step One: Receiving Forgiveness.*

An elderly lady in my congregation was driving to the store on a cold and busy Saturday morning. With lots of errands ahead of her, she wanted to grab her milk and bananas first thing. The traffic on the way to the store was busier than usual, but she made it. Electing to go back a different way, she pulled out into the busy street, just dodging an oncoming car.

To her dismay (and embarrassment!), she realized she had pulled out in front of a parade float. She had swung her Oldsmobile in front of Santa's sled in the town Christmas parade! The mayor and a local congressman were in the float ahead of her with Saint Nick in the rearview.

There is a naive assumption among spiritual people (even Christians) that we can casually glide in and out of the presence of God, as if you can simply pull into the presence of the Lord of Hosts like my friend with the parade. But the Scriptures teach us that the presence of God is a holy, frightful place. You cannot just drift into his throne room.

When Moses was summoned to the top of Mount Sinai to receive the Ten Commandments, God turned his back to him, lest the full weight of his glory destroy the mortal servant.[2]

Isaiah came before God in a vision and immediately felt overwhelmed by the holiness of God. An angel put a burning coal on his lips as a sign of purification.[3]

In the tabernacle of the Old Testament (and later the Temple), the holy of holies was the inner sanctum where the glory of God dwelt. A large curtain separated the holy of holies from the rest of the complex. The priest was allowed to enter one day a year (the Day of Atonement) and only after a long series of purification rituals. Should a priest enter without ritual cleansing, the holiness of God would overwhelm the priest, and he would die.[4]

In each instance, the holy grandeur of God engulfs those who stand in his presence. God allows people to enter his presence, but only after a covering or purification has been made. God is holy, and in our sinful condition, we are unable to experience his glory without some sort of covering.

Because God is holy, our sin is intolerable. Anything that is impure or blemished cannot dwell in his presence. If God were a lesser being, sin would not be an issue. But he is God: eternal, majestic, and holy. Yet God is also loving and desires to commune with his fallen creation. The Bible is, in part, a story of how God offered various means of reconciliation to himself.

In the Old Testament, he revealed to his people how to cover their sins through ritual sacrifice. But the ritual was incomplete. The sacrifices had to be made in perpetuity. Added to that, the Temple and its religious orders became corrupted. Priests abused their power, and the Hebrews failed to acknowledge the gravity of the rituals. Some followed the commands of God just to impress their peers. Still others followed the Law to the letter, but became hard-hearted and ignored the plight of the poor. The prophets foretold a coming Messiah, a chosen One of God, who would fulfill the law and restore holy worship.

When Jesus died on the cross, he was a perfect sacrifice. His shed blood served as a covering for the sins of all who would receive him.[5] The crucifixion was not just the death of a failed revolutionary or the silencing of another prophet. Jesus taught his disciples that he would serve as a "ransom for many."[6]

Under the old covenant, God required an animal sacrifice, the blood of which would act as a covering for sin. During the Passover, the Hebrew people were required to paint blood on their doorposts so the angel of death would "pass over" their homes. The blood was the covering from judgment.

On Calvary, under God's new covenant, the shed blood of Jesus is the covering for our sin. Because of his sacrifice, we can approach the throne of God:

> *Let us then approach God's throne of grace with confidence, so that we may receive mercy and find grace to help us in our time of need.*[7]

When Jesus died, the curtain in the Temple, which separated the holy of holies from the rest of the courts, was torn in two from top to bottom.[8] As Jesus gave up his life, the barrier that once kept us from the holiness of God was removed. In Christ, our sins are covered and we can approach the throne of grace.

The First Word Was a Prayer

The first cry of the cross was a prayer. It is fitting that Jesus would offer a prayer while on the cross. His life and ministry were saturated with prayer. He prayed in solitude during the most hectic season of ministry.[9] Before he fed the masses through the miraculous act of multiplying bread and fish, Jesus offered a prayer of thanksgiving.[10] The high priestly prayer found in John's gospel gives us a glimpse into the intimacy Jesus shared with God the Father.[11] His prayers in Gethsemane were so fervent that he sweat blood.[12] Jesus taught his disciples how to pray. The Lord's Prayer is both a stand-alone prayer and a template to shape our discourse with God.[13] He taught about humility and sincerity in prayer, instead of babbling in public to gain attention.[14] Prayer in the quiet places, with the door shut, expresses the true desires of the heart.[15]

On the cross, Jesus was in a desperate situation, and a desperate prayer would be in order. Our Savior was familiar with desperation: a father pleading for his dying daughter; a woman, bleeding and flat broke, longing for healing.[16] Even a banquet master who ran out of wine led to a desperate request for Jesus![17]

Prayers of desperation are as old as time. Looking to the heavens for help in dark hours is a practice among all peoples through all time. We do not have to be taught to say desperate prayers. The other criminals who were crucified that day were saying prayers as well to someone, somewhere. The old aphorism is true: there are no atheists in foxholes. In the darkest hours, even the staunchest atheist calls out to someone…anyone…for help.

Desperate prayers are the most sincere. The most fervent prayers are after the dire diagnosis, when the child storms out, or after the latest round of layoffs at work. During the mundane times, we have to search for things to say to God. But when we are betrayed and abandoned, we do not lack the words. We cry out for help. For rescue. For an answer. For deliverance.

Jesus prayed in his time of desperation, but not for relief. He prayed for the people who were persecuting him. In our hours of desperation and disillusion, our first desire is relief from the affliction. Yet Jesus spent his first moments in prayer and, as we will see, he did not pray for relief. He prayed to a God who was close to him in his affliction and for the enemies who had brought the suffering upon him.

"Father": The first word of Jesus from the cross was to his Father. A word from Jesus to his father is fitting. Jesus began his ministry with a word from the Father to the Son. At his baptism, God the Father spoke:

> *This is my Son, whom I love; with him I am well pleased.*[18]

The Father who spoke to initiate his ministry was now listening as his Son completed his work on Calvary.

When he addressed God the Father at the outset, we are reminded that all creation, life, and death spring from the heart of the Father. God is the center of all things. The Bible is a recollection of his care and providence over his people, and all creation will one day submit before him. In an age of selfie booths in ultra-hip, convenient megachurches, we should remember that faith is not about our "experience." Our worship is about God the Father. He is the king of all creation. Again, the holiness of God is such that no person can stand before him without being overcome by his majesty.

Which brings us to the sheer audacity of Jesus calling him "Father" from the cross. To call God "Father" would have been scandalous in its own right. The name of God was revered, and many Hebrews would not dare utter his name. To say his name with mere human language was to diminish his grandeur. When Moses sought to hear the name of God so he could tell the Hebrew people who was sending him, God said "I am that I am."[19] This is a title that reflects the eternity and profundity of the living God.

In the Old Testament, there are a few instances when God refers to himself in more personal terms. But the typical title for God was "Lord," the name that subjects call their master.

That is why, when Jesus had the temerity to say, "The Father and I are One,"[20] the religious authorities knew they had a solid case for blasphemy. Jesus went even further and taught his disciples to pray, "Our Father...who is in heaven."[21]

Though it was offensive to the religious class, Jesus taught us that God is a father. He is family. We are his children. God has a heart for his beloved. He is not a staunch rule-giver waiting to punish his creation. God has the familial love that a parent has for his child.

There is a famous picture of President Kennedy walking out of church with secret service men on both sides. It was a tense time in our nation's history, and JFK was likely chatting about his upcoming agenda. Civil rights, unrest, and the Cold War were weighing on the national consciousness. President Kennedy had very important decisions to make that would affect millions of people. His actions would affect the course of American history.

A closer look at that picture reveals what the president was holding in his hands: a baby doll! His daughter was walking in front with a chipper smile. She knew nothing of the weight of the world on her daddy's shoulders. Little Caroline Kennedy was playing with a doll, got tired of carrying it, and handed it over to her daddy without thinking twice. As parents know, kids don't just plop down their baby dolls; they need to be handled with care. And every dad in the world has been handed a toy. (At least I have, at least a million times!) Sure, John Kennedy was president of the United States and his nation was on the brink of war. But someone called him daddy and handed him their toys.

What an honor to know that the God of the universe, who has authority far beyond any king or president, is also our father. From the cross, Jesus cried out to his father. This cry from the cross is a reminder that God has a deep and abiding love for us. As Jesus said, "Which of you, if your son asks for bread, will give him a stone?"[22] When we come to him in our desperation, we receive the tender care of a parent. We come to God, not as subjects, but as his children.

"Forgive": Jesus's plea to his father was to forgive those who were persecuting him. The first word is not an exasperated, exhausted plea for help. This prayer is not even about himself. When he was suffering the excruciating humiliation of the cross, his mind turned to others. He prayed for the forgiveness of his persecutors. How many times have you prayed for the person who has harmed you? In your hour of desperation, have you prayed for the deliverance of the person who put you in that situation? If we're being honest, our minds do not usually leap to the defense of those who have offended us. Quite the opposite.

Jesus's prayer from the cross mirrors his life and teachings. Forgiveness is the central theme of his ministry:

> *But I tell you, love your enemies and pray*
> *for those who persecute you, that you may*
> *be children of your Father in heaven.*[23]

When he taught his disciples to pray, they were to expect forgiveness from God only inasmuch as they had forgiven others.[24] When Peter was looking for an actual number of times he had to forgive someone else, Jesus told him seventy times seven, implying that he needed to forgive so much he'd lose count![25]

In the parable of the unmerciful servant, Jesus warned against receiving forgiveness of a great debt without offering that forgiveness to others. The most familiar parable about forgiveness is the parable of the prodigal son.[26] Recognizing his sin and tired of being estranged from his father, the prodigal returned home and was welcomed, and forgiven, by his father. Forgiveness is at the heart of the ministry of Jesus, so it is no surprise that his first words from the agony of the cross were a plea for his persecutors.

The prophet Isaiah foretold of the suffering Messiah who would pray for his enemies while bearing their sins:

> *For he bore the sin of many, and made intercession for the transgressors.*[27]

Jesus fulfilled this prophecy by bearing the sin of the world and praying for the people who had put him on the cross. Jesus continues the ministry of intercession for us, as expressed by the writer of Hebrews:

> *Therefore he is able to save completely those who come to God through him, because he always lives to intercede for them.*[28]

As we hear this first statement from the cross, we are reminded of the importance of forgiveness in the Christian life. Those of us who have been forgiven of such great debts must, in turn, forgive others. The Christian capacity to forgive, rather than seek revenge, is the marker of a regenerated life. The natural tendency of fallen humanity is to take back what is ours. When we are wronged, we want to recover what was lost, and usually some more. Christ both preached and practiced forgiveness. Those who follow his Way are compelled to do the same.

But the act of forgiveness is always difficult. When we are offended, we tend to hold those grievances very close. Those who have done the offending are no longer people; they are villains, and it is hard for us to forget that moniker.

When thinking about the difficulty in forgiving, our minds may jump to those extreme scenarios. The parents struggling to forgive the drunk driver who harmed their child. The adulterous husband or the drug-addicted assaulter. Offering forgiveness in those situations is a difficult, complex, and personal process.

If we are being honest, the offenses we endure and the bitterness we harbor are usually less consequential. Those who need our forgiveness are rarely those who have offended us in big ways, but in the small nuances of life. The critical boss or the gossipy coworker. The family member who offends us over the holidays. The neglectful spouse. The church bully. Much of our time and emotional energy are poured into analyzing the various, usually inconsequential, offenses levied at us every day. Do large-scale, life-altering offenses happen? Of course. But the majority of the offenses against us are relatively small.

Jesus was often offended by his disciples. They were impulsive, often lacked faith,[29] and obtuse.[30] They bickered with one another.[31] And yet Jesus endured with them. His presence was an act of forgiveness. When we tire of people, we tend to move on to the next friendship. But Jesus labored with his disciples.

The disciples, who Jesus loved and forgave, abandoned him in his most desperate hour. While he was crucified, the gospels report only one disciple (John) was there to witness it.[32] The others had fled. This was no small offense. This was betrayal. It is one thing to be harmed; it is another to be betrayed. Your enemies will harm you, but only your friends betray you.

Jesus forgave in the big offenses as he did in the small. His life was wrapped in grace. Likewise, we will not be able to forgive the great offenders in our lives unless we start with the mundane, everyday grievances. Jesus said, "Whoever can be trusted with very little can also be trusted with much."[33] This applies to forgiveness. If we cannot forgive the less consequential grievances, then we will certainly not be able to forgive those who have harmed us the most. Jesus is our model of forgiveness. He forgave people at every turn and, when the greatest offense came, he said without hesitation, "Father, forgive them." With enough time and experience in the presence of Christ and, with God's help, perhaps we can learn to wrap our lives in grace as well.

Why Did Jesus Ask His Father to Forgive?

This statement from Jesus raises an important question: Why did Jesus ask his Father to forgive them? He has the power and authority to forgive sin. He is God; the second person in the Godhead. They were crucifying him because Jesus (rightly) claimed his authority to forgive sin. To the paralyzed man, he said, "Son, your sins are forgiven."[34] When a less-than-virtuous woman came to wash the feet of Jesus, he said, "Your sins are forgiven."[35] He made the same proclamation to the paralytic, "Take heart, son; your sins are forgiven."[36] If Jesus had the power to forgive, why did he ask his father to do the forgiving?

The answer is that Jesus was asking on behalf of beleaguered humanity. The cross revealed Jesus at his "most human." He was enduring the suffering, shame, betrayal, and torment that come with bearing sin-ridden flesh. On the cross, Jesus took on the frail and mortal flesh of humanity. He became as we are. It is fitting then, that he would ask God to forgive, as a plea on behalf of humanity. As God, Jesus can forgive sins, heal the sick, and perceive hearts. In the flesh, seen most vividly on the cross, he suffered and cried out to God with the rest of fallen humanity.

The Depths of Sin

Sin is no small matter. The crucifixion is a stark reminder of the consequences of sin. Some contend that, because God is so loving and gracious, he will simply ignore sin or weigh it against good deeds: as if God is a divine bureaucrat, carefully calculating offense and virtue.

But try as we might, sin cannot be underestimated. The human condition is permeated with sin, which creates an impregnable divide between God and his creation. God, who is all holy, cannot tolerate the sin that engulfs our existence. The wages of our sin is death.[37] And, left uncovered, we stand condemned in our sinful state.

Sin not only creates division between God and humanity, but sin causes divisions among people. The residual effect of sin is discord, violence, poverty, and societal brokenness. Sin causes the disparity of wealth and power so prevalent through human history. Sin creates injustice. The bloody brutality of the cross of Calvary, committed by people who were certain of their civility and righteousness, is a picture of the confusion and disillusion of the sinful condition.

The punishment for our sin is painful condemnation. When Jesus bore our sin and received punishment, it was not a light sentence. The pain and torment of the cross was the burden he had to bear to carry the punishment we deserved. Such is the gravity of sin.

"Them": Jesus prayed to his Father that he would forgive "them." But who were they? Did they want to be forgiven? This was no generic request on the part of Jesus. There were people, literally right below him in that moment, who were killing him. And yet he prayed for "them."

Who was Jesus praying for? He had a number of enemies, all of whom directly or indirectly contributed to his sentencing:

Religious leaders: The ministry of Jesus was popular for a number of reasons, all of which were threatening to the religious establishment of the day. Jesus offended the Pharisees, who insisted on strict religious observance for themselves and others. They frequently gossiped about Jesus from afar and frequently criticized him for a supposed lack of religious decorum. While the people of Israel were spiritually neglected and suffering injustice, the Pharisees were worried about proper hand washing.[38]

Jesus offended the Sadducees, who were a smaller but similarly important sect of religious Jews. They were typically in a higher social standing, and they were more influenced by Greek philosophy. The Sadducees were an aristocratic sort. Jesus was an equal-opportunity offender. He offended the religious sensibilities of the Sadducees by confounding them with his wisdom and failing to fall into their theological traps.[39] They would not be disrespected by a bumpkin peasant from Galilee. The Sadducees and Pharisees, normally foes in their social and theological outlook, found a common enemy in Jesus of Nazareth. They would conspire to bring charges that would eventually lead to the cross.

And yet, while on Calvary, Jesus prayed for them. He prayed for those religious elites who were certain in their religious convictions yet remained callous to the injustices of the world. I wish I could say this fickle spirituality died with the Pharisees and Sadducees. But sadly, most of the church bullies I have confronted in my travels in ministry are not those who are new to the faith and eager to sit at the feet of Christ. The modern-day "local religious leaders" keep an air of certainty and, though frequently wrong about their assertions, they are never in doubt.

On the cross, Jesus was praying for those who let religion and rituals supersede their relationship with God. Like the Pharisees and Sadducees, people will convince themselves of their spiritual worth by performing religious rituals. In Jesus's day, it was proper hand-washing and strict fasting. In our day, it's making sure the church carpet color stays the same and the sacred cows are never moved. It's all cut from the same cloth. The good news is Jesus prays for everyone who has lost their focus and become too religious for their own good.

Civil government: The Roman occupation made Israel a political hotbed. The Roman peace came at the end of a sword. The empire had little patience for the rebellion that was always stirring underneath the surface. Its agents were quick to make a public display of anyone who would disrupt the fragile social order.

The religious leaders who brought charges against Jesus accused him of "blasphemy." They knew these charges would carry weight with the Romans, not because their occupiers had the same theological convictions, but because they knew a blasphemer could cause a stir among the local population. The Romans did not want any noise from a Galilean prophet that would challenge the social order. So, when the charges were brought against Jesus, they made haste to execute. There was some lip service paid to justice. They gave him a hearing before the Sanhedrin and an audience with Pilate.[40] The Roman prelate then asked the mob what they wanted to do. Not exactly law and order.

And yet Jesus prayed for their forgiveness. He prayed for the state actors who were committing the greatest injustice in history. The course of human history is wrought with corruption from the state. Governments are just as sinful and fallen as those they govern. The poor are always the first victims of injustice. The "trial" of Jesus was one in a long line of the powerful bringing injustice upon the poor. This prayer for forgiveness makes us long for a perfect kingdom where justice reigns.

Disciples: Jesus loved his disciples. They were close to his heart. He called them to discipleship and showed them the kingdom. And they loved him, too, while it was convenient. They liked being his entourage when he was performing miracles and standing up to the religious elite. But when Jesus was in his hour of desperation, the disciples fled. They had let him down before. But this was different. Jesus was literally dying, and every disciple, with one exception, left him in his time of need.[41] They betrayed Jesus.

Perhaps this is the most remarkable aspect of the prayer for "them." The religious leaders were predictable in their opposition to Jesus. The state is always a self-interested actor; of course its agents were going to convict the innocent man. But his disciples? His friends? These are the same people who swore allegiance to him the night before and promised to never leave. Now they were gone. Still, Jesus prayed for them.

Of course, none of us like to imagine ourselves as the ones who would betray Jesus. We would never abandon him. But we are kidding ourselves. We make broad, passionate claims of our love for Jesus in Sunday worship, but neglect him throughout the week. We believe in the doctrines and can recite the creeds, but we are just as prone to sin in the hour of temptation. Of course we would betray Jesus.

But he continues to pray for us. He intercedes for us. He continues to forgive. This cry from the cross is a reminder of the incredible depth of his love for us.

"For they know not what they do": As Jesus prayed for the forgiveness of his enemies, there was an added measure of grace. Jesus asked for pardon for everyone who was culpable because "they know not what they do." This portion of the prayer seems contradictory: of course they knew what they were doing! The religious leaders had been plotting for months. The Romans had perfected the torment and torture of the execution. The disciples made a calculated decision to run away.

As Jesus was praying from the cross, he knew something that we, in our limited minds, cannot fathom. Jesus's connection with the Father, his perfect obedience, and the burden of the cross are beyond our intellectual grasp. We simply cannot understand the glory of Christ or appreciate the depths of sin that nailed him to the cross. The characters depicted in the passion narrative were acting out of self-interest. Everyone thought they were doing God's work. The religious leaders were silencing a blasphemer. The soldiers, who beat and nailed him to the tree, were just doing their jobs. The Roman authorities were keeping the peace. The disciples were saving their skins. Everyone did what they thought was right. But, as they went through the motions and allowed Christ to bear the cross, they were blind to the depths of their depravity and the complex beauty of God's plan.

Those who crucified Jesus had an obviously limited knowledge of the consequences of their actions. And yet they acted with certainty. Part of the lesson of this first word from the cross is that there is much we do not know. In our limited scope, we contend to possess great knowledge, but we are only a flicker compared with the vast omniscience of God. What was true in the Garden of Eden remains: our greatest temptation is to share the knowledge of our Creator.

The first temptation in the Garden of Eden was for humanity to know what God knows. The serpent tried (successfully) to sway Adam and Eve into disobedience by cajoling them to bite the forbidden fruit. When Satan tempted, he told them they would "be like God, knowing good and evil."[42] Satan did not tempt them with power, authority, or wealth. Rather, the first couple was tempted into disobedience because they craved the divine knowledge.

A few chapters later, fallen humanity sought to build a tower into the heavens to bridge the divide between the mortal and immortal.[43] They wanted to witness the things of God, though they were mere mortals. Later still, King Saul went so far as to consult a witch to know the future that God had for him.[44]

There are many modern manifestations of the corrupted desire for knowledge. Televangelists promise restored health (a bright future!) for a few bucks. There is an unsettling rise in paganism, witchcraft, and nature worship, each with promises of glimpses into the mystical unknown. The desire to know that which only God can know is a primal temptation. Those who crucified Jesus did so without hesitation because they "knew" it was right for them to do. How wrong they were.

The first statement from the cross is full of grace. He was forgiving to his enemies who both betrayed him and brought terrible physical pain. His forgiveness is beautiful because those who were killing him were doing so in obtuse ignorance. Those at the cross could see the reality of the nails and blood only in their limited scope. In that moment, they knew what they were doing. But they could not fathom the egregiousness of their offense against God. Jesus is perfectly obedient, and God is wholly righteous. Fallen humanity was humiliating, torturing, and killing the Chosen of God and doing so with confidence that they were righteous actors. What ignorance! And yet Jesus cried out, "Forgive…for they know not what they do." Could we forgive in such a way? Could we forgive those offenses that deeply sting our hearts? Could we assume the best intentions of those around us and forgive the callous ignorance of those who offend us? We tend to carry grudges far too long. The smallest grievances stay with us. What if we forgave like Jesus and asked…or begged… God to forgive those who trespass against us?

Step One: Receiving Forgiveness is essential to be in a relationship with God. We know God because he offers forgiveness through the shed blood of Jesus. At the cross, we are made aware of the great mercy of Jesus. Even while he suffered, he prayed for the forgiveness of his persecutors. As we come into relationship with God through Jesus Christ, we become compelled to offer forgiveness to others, just as we have received mercy from God.

---

[1] 1 John 4:19
[2] Exodus 33:13
[3] Isaiah 6:7-13
[4] Leviticus 10:2-3
[5] John 1:12
[6] Mark 10:45
[7] Hebrews 4:16
[8] Matthew 27:51
[9] Luke 5:16
[10] Matthew 14:19
[11] John 17:1-26
[12] John 19:24-25
[13] Matthew 6:9-13, Luke 11:2-4
[14] Matthew 6:7
[15] Matthew 6:6
[16] Luke 8:40-56
[17] John 2:3
[18] Matthew 3:17
[19] Exodus 3:14
[20] John 10:30
[21] Matthew 6:7
[22] Matthew 7:9
[23] Matthew 5:44-45a
[24] Matthew 6:14-15

[25] Matthew 18:21-22
[26] Luke 15:11-32
[27] Isaiah 53:12
[28] Hebrews 7:25
[29] Mark 4:35-41
[30] Luke 18:34
[31] Luke 9:46
[32] John 19:25
[33] Luke 16:10
[34] Mark 2:5
[35] Luke 7:48
[36] Matthew 9:2
[37] Romans 6:23
[38] Matthew 15:2
[39] Matthew 22:23-46
[40] Matthew 26:57-67
[41] John 19:24
[42] Genesis 3:5
[43] Genesis 11:1-9
[44] 1 Samuel 28

Step Two - Citizens of a New Kingdom

"Truly I tell you, today you will be with me in paradise."
Luke 23:43

On a sunny day in July 2006, Emily and I stood at the altar of marriage and pledged our devotion to one another. We repeated traditional Quaker wedding vows:

> *...promising, with Divine Assistance, to be unto thee, a loving and faithful husband/ wife as long as we both shall live.*

We exchanged rings and an awkward smooch and were pronounced husband and wife. We processed down the aisle to applause and a piano rendition of the "Doxology." It was a beautiful day. We were off to "happily ever after."

Could you imagine if, once we reached the doors of the church, Emily and I parted ways, never to speak again? As if she were to go her way, and I were to go mine. What if we made this grand proclamation of our love and commitment only to separate a few moments later? That thought is absurd, of course. And, thankfully, Emily and I have continued to grow together in our marriage.

Step One: Receiving Forgiveness marks our union with God. We have received forgiveness and entered into relationship with him. We have made a pronouncement of our devotion to him. But our newfound relationship with God is just the first step in a long walk with him. Just as Emily and I have grown closer since our wedding, so too, the believer should pursue a deeper life with God after conversion. The second word from the cross reveals the next stage of our spiritual journey. In *Step Two: Citizens of a New Kingdom*, we enter a new phase in our journey with him. We become citizens of a new kingdom.

Kingdom Citizens

Once forgiven and saved by the atoning work of Christ on the cross, Christians join the Kingdom of God. Receiving Christ and the promise of heaven does not mark the end of the journey. It is the beginning. Christians are called to a new way of life that reflects the desire of God. Jesus taught his followers to reflect the ideals of heaven, such as love, mercy, and justice, here on earth. "When you pray," Jesus said, we should plead for the work of heaven to be done on earth: "Your Kingdom come, your will be done…on earth as it is in heaven."[1]

The Kingdom of Heaven is a central theme in the teaching and preaching of Jesus. The term "kingdom" (Βασίλειο) is used more than 150 times in the New Testament, fifty-six times in the gospel of Matthew alone. The bulk of Jesus's parables begin with "the kingdom of heaven is like…" The "kingdom" teachings of Jesus direct the believer to God and his sovereign reign over the world. Because the world is fallen, not everyone will enter or enjoy the kingdom of God. Those who follow Christ are now citizens of this kingdom. Kingdom citizens live by a different "rule," one of forgiveness, kindness, and mercy. Christians continue to live on earth, under temporal secular authorities, but they have an inward, spiritual allegiance to the Kingdom of God. Later in the New Testament, Peter reminds the fledgling church of its true identity:

> *But you are a chosen people, a royal priesthood, a holy nation, God's special possession, that you may declare the praises of him who called you out of darkness into his wonderful light. Once you were not a people, but now you are the people of God; once you had not received mercy, but now you have received mercy.*[2]

We tend to associate heaven with the afterlife. But Jesus teaches us that kingdom ideals should be lived on earth. We are called to Christ and his kingdom in the here and now. We can enjoy the paradise of God in this life. Our sinful condition does not allow us to grasp the majesty of God's presence, but we can taste the goodness of God nonetheless. When we come in to Christ, we are given a glimpse of our eternity with God. Paul articulated this idea in a letter to the Corinthian church: "Now I know in part; then I shall know fully, even as I am fully known."[3] Paul was leaning into the mystery of the divine. No, we cannot know God in his fullness in this life, but in Christ we are granted entry to paradise. We are given a taste of eternity and the paradise to follow!

When we accept Christ, we convert from our old life into a new walk with Christ and enter into a kingdom life. This means accepting the call to discipleship under Christ and living as a citizen of his kingdom. We begin to live by his rule and Way. The teachings of Jesus become the focal point of the Christian life.

In this chapter, we will meet criminals who supported a failed revolution. They sought to expel the Roman occupiers. But their cause met a swift end. That is the way it usually goes. Movements come and go. Empires rise and fall. But the Christian who enters the kingdom life becomes part of a movement that lasts into eternity.

The Second Word

The second word from the cross is in response to a criminal who accepts his guilt. It is the only word from the cross that comes from dialogue with someone else. This chapter is going to focus on the conversation that led to Jesus's words:

> *Truly I tell you, today you will be with me in Paradise.*[4]

We understand this statement only when we hear the criminal who evoked these precious words from Jesus.

There is a classic scene in the movie *The Shawshank Redemption*.[5] Andy Dufresne has been convicted of murder and begins to settle into prison life. As he is meeting some of the other inmates, he befriends another prisoner, Red, and asks for his help in smuggling in some contraband. This sets off a very funny scene.

Red says to Andy, "[You are] the wife-killing banker. Why'd you do it?" To which Andy replies, "I didn't, since you asked." Red laughs and says, "You're gonna fit right in! Everybody in here is innocent. Didn't you know that?" The seasoned prisoner asks another inmate why he is in prison. He gets the immediate reply, "Didn't do it!"

The running joke among prisoners is everyone is behind bars, but no one is guilty. They are all convicted and serving time, but no one admits their crime. We find this scene funny because we all have the same inclination to hide our faults.

I have had similar experiences with actual prisoners. In hours of counsel and Bible study in jails, few have admitted their fault in the crimes that led them to conviction. They often refuse to accept full responsibility for their actions. They scoff at the victim or blame the system. Anything to shirk their guilt.

The second word from the cross comes after a sincere plea from someone we will come to know as the Good Thief. This criminal acknowledged both his guilt and the authority of Jesus. For this simple confession, he was welcomed into paradise. Jesus addressed a condemned criminal from the cross and offered eternal security. The second word is a comforting sign of God's unending mercy to a fallen world.

There were two criminals crucified at the right and left of Jesus on the hill called Golgotha.[6] One criminal, known as the Scoffer, heaped scorn on Jesus and showed no remorse. The Good Thief pled guilty and acknowledged Jesus as Lord. Both criminals had been working toward a revolution that failed. The kingdom they imagined, free from Roman rule, would not arrive in their lifetimes. But in his anguish, the Good Thief saw a greater kingdom manifest in Jesus. His confession teaches us about our opportunity to enter the Kingdom of Heaven.

Jesus among the Convicts

The Son of God was crucified between criminals and crowds of onlookers scoffing at him. Only days before, these same folks were calling him "Hosanna."[7] Now they were mocking him as life bled away. During the height of his popularity, Jesus had people clamor to be at his side. The disciples once argued over who would get to be at his right and left.[8] At the transfiguration, Moses and

Elijah appeared by his side. But on Calvary, those on his right and left were convicted criminals. More than 700 years earlier, Isaiah prophesied that the Messiah would be "numbered with the transgressors."[9] Jesus confirmed this grim prophecy:

> ...*and I tell you that this must be fulfilled in me. Yes, what is written about me is reaching its fulfillment.*[10]

It is fitting that Jesus would die among the dregs of society. He spent his life with those on the fringes. He kept company with prostitutes, tax collectors, and all manner of sinners.[11] The reason he was despised by the religious elite was his elbow-rubbing with the lower sort. A true prophet, they surmised, would never consort with the unrighteous.[12] But Jesus came to seek and to save the lost.[13] The poor were privy to the first riches of the kingdom. Jesus lived among the lowly. He was born among beasts in a manger; now he was dying among the beasts of society.

The two condemned to die next to Jesus were no common criminals. The Romans had a variety of punishments for lawbreakers: jail, beheading, and forced slavery, just to name a few. The crucifixion was a melding of punishment, torment, and shame. It was reserved for those who threatened the social order of the Roman peace. These criminals were likely revolutionaries, people who would fight and die to rid Israel of Roman occupation. The criminals crucified on both sides of Jesus are often referred to as "thieves," because the Greek word translated léstés (λῃστής) has multiple meanings. It can be translated into a number of words, from common thief to marauder. One concordance says a léstés is an "unscrupulous marauder (malefactor), exploiting the vulnerable without hesitating to use violence."[14] Whatever their crimes, they had done something noteworthy to raise the ire of the occupying powers. These were tough characters.

The Scoffer

The old saying, "There is no honor among thieves" was true on the first Good Friday. The public execution of Jesus was a frightful and brutal scene that revealed the harshness of the human heart. It was not enough to convict Jesus, flog, strip, and spit on him. They had to hurl insults, too. A criminal who was crucified next to Jesus began to scoff at Jesus:

> *Aren't you the Messiah? Save yourself and us.*[15]

Misery loves company. This criminal was doing his best to make sure that everyone's suffering was as painful as possible. It is a telling account of this unnamed man. We like to think that, at our final moments, we will be at our best. But this man was dying as he likely lived: with bitterness and contempt.

The Scoffer had a narrow view. In his final moments, he was following the pack and ridiculing Jesus. There was no self-reflection or compassion. Unbeknownst to him, the mockery of the Scoffer hit an important theological point. He was asking Jesus to do the one thing he could not do in this moment: save himself. Jesus came to suffer and die for the sins of the world.[16] If Jesus were to "save himself" by coming down from the cross, the world would stand condemned. Jesus has the authority to command legions of angels.[17] Jesus stood toe-to-toe with the devil and resisted his temptations.[18] Jesus's strength and authority are not in question. Yet to win the battle over death, Jesus had to suffer death.

The Good Thief

The other criminal takes a different tone. Both criminals are called "thieves," but only one had a change of heart and receives the positive moniker. There is much speculation surrounding the identity of the Good Thief, most of it the product of legend and speculation. Western Christendom remembers him as Dismas and honors him on March 25, alongside the Feast of Annunciation. In art and literature, he is contrasted with the Scoffer because, as we'll see, he made a stunning confession about Jesus.

We know enough about the Good Thief to make some important conclusions. Like his counterpart, the Good Thief was likely a rough character. Jesus was crucified because he was deemed a threat to the Jewish religious authorities and hence the Roman peace. If his message spread, his followers may have upended the social order. Jesus never took up a sword or advocated violence. But many of the revolutionaries did. They were ready and willing to spill blood. We can infer that the Scoffer and Good Thief had either acted in violence or were plotting to do so.

Matthew's gospel records both mocked Jesus.[19] But the Good Thief had a change of heart. In his pain and suffering, the criminal spoke to his fellow condemned:

> *Don't you fear God, since you are under the same sentence?*[20]

This simple statement was a retort to the Scoffer. The Good Thief told the Scoffer that he had no place to mock Jesus. God's justice had come down on all of them. We never hear from the Scoffer again.

The Good Thief continued:

> *We are punished justly, for we are getting what we deserve. But this man has done nothing wrong.*[21]

This passage highlights the great change that occurred within the Good Thief. He admitted his crimes. No one else in the scene from the Scoffer to the soldiers to the crowd had a moment of self-reflection. They did not consider their wrongdoing. Everyone assumed they were doing the good and just thing. Even their mockery completed the deserved punishment of Jesus and the other criminals. But the Good Thief had a moment of clarity and inward change. All at once, he recognized the hypocrisy of the Scoffer, the weight of his guilt, and the significance of Christ crucified.

When we hear the Good Thief say, "This man has done nothing wrong," we are reminded of Pilate, who said the same thing of Jesus. Jesus had an audience with the Roman governor and, in a short conversation, Pilate was convinced of the rabbi's innocence. Like the Good Thief, Pilate proclaimed to the angry mob, "I find no basis for a charge against this man."[22] Still the horde wanted blood. Pilate literally and figuratively "washed his hands" of any wrongdoing and turned Jesus over to his executioners.[23] When he recognized the innocence of Jesus, Pilate sought to alleviate his own guilt. When the Good Thief recognized the innocence of Jesus, he opened his heart in confession and repentance. We are beginning to see why he is called the "Good" Thief!

The Cry of the Good Thief

Recognizing his own guilt and the innocence of Jesus, the Good Thief continued:

> *Jesus, remember me when you come into your kingdom.*[24]

"Jesus": Notice how the Good Thief used Jesus's proper name. Throughout his ministry, Jesus was called many things, by friends and foes alike. They called him "good teacher," Rabbi, Lord, Master, Son of David…even Hosanna (which means "our God saves"). Only sick and afflicted people called him "Jesus." Before his entry into Jerusalem, the only people who actually called Jesus by his first name were his family.[25]

Author James Martin speculates that Jesus may have liked hearing his first name.[26] Perhaps it reminded him of simpler days in the presence of his friends and family. The obvious effect of the cross is how it stripped away all titles and pretense. Pain and death have a way of doing that. On Calvary, Jesus was bearing all the suffering of humanity without an aura of divinity. The Good Thief could not yet see the glory of Christ. He saw another suffering human. No wonder he called him by his first name.

The use of his proper name reveals that the Good Thief was not a man of spiritual refinement, nor had he heard of Jesus before the crucifixion. He had already recognized Jesus as innocent, which for a Jew is synonymous with "blameless" and "righteous"; terms reserved for their greatest heroes. But the Good Thief either does not know or care to use those expressions. The Good Thief lacked religious decorum and vocabulary.

"Remember me": The Good Thief did not ask for glory or power. Unlike the disciples, he did not ask to sit at a place of honor with Jesus when he came into his kingdom.[27] He just did not want to be forgotten. The Good Thief made a powerful statement about the character of God. Throughout the Old Testament, God declared over and again that he will not forget his children.[28]

Further still, God tells his children not to forget him. He has chosen his people for a special purpose, to receive the Law and share his covenant with the world. Whenever God made a decree or proclamation, it usually began with a reminder, "I am the Lord your God, who brought you out of slavery."[29] The children of God are not forgotten, and they should not forget his salvation.

By saying "remember me," the Good Thief was asking to be among the chosen of God. Acknowledging his sin and guilt, he recognized Jesus as the bearer of God's covenant and asked only to be remembered.

Deathbed Conversion

The Good Thief has been a source of comfort because his last-minute confession opens the possibility of a deathbed conversion. We can continue to pray for our friends and family members who continue to reject Jesus, even late in life. We can have hope that, even in their last breath, they could accept Jesus as Savior. The Good Thief converts in his final moments. Maybe those close to us will do the same.

On the other side of the coin, some believe they can live however they like and accept Christ in their last breath and receive their eternal reward. This is foolish, as no one knows their last moment of life. To hold off conversion until the last moment is playing with fire. People who reject Christ in the good times of life will likely reject him as they near death. One Puritan author had good insight when he said of this passage, "There is one such case recorded that none need despair, but only one that none might presume."[30]

Warren Wiersbe notes that the Good Thief does not wait until the last moment to accept Christ. Rather, he converts at his first opportunity![31] He had never heard a sermon or witnessed a miracle. His first encounter with Jesus was from the cross, and he received him right away.

"When you come into your kingdom": Though his moments on earth were waning, the Good Thief had a vision of the future. He sensed that Jesus would reign in a kingdom beyond the cross. He was right. When in the torment of pain and suffering, we are rarely able to think about the future. But at the side of Jesus, the Good Thief had a hopeful vision. The revolution had failed. There would be no restored kingdom brought about by war. Perhaps the Good Thief perceived a truth that so few recognize: that every revolution, empire, nation, and authority on earth will disappear. They will be whisked away with the sands of time: "The grass withers and the flowers fall…Surely the people are grass."[32] The Good Thief laid down his defenses and surrendered his notion of an earthly revolution. He joined an eternal kingdom.

Why the Change of Heart?

What brought about this great change? Why did the Good Thief have a change of heart while the Scoffer continued in his misery? There are a few clues in the gospels.

While he was suffering next to Jesus, he heard him forgive his enemies. Perhaps the Good Thief was heart struck by Jesus's merciful sermon: "Father, forgive them, for they know not what they do."

Those mocking him called Jesus the "Son of God," who has the power to save himself and others. Maybe the Good Thief read between the lines and recognized the truth underneath the mockery. Jesus does indeed have the power to save.

Pilate ordered a sign posted above Jesus's head, intended as mockery, which read: "This is the King of the Jews."[33] Wiersbe calls this the first "gospel tract," as it identifies the reign of Jesus.[34] Maybe the Good Thief read it literally.

We cannot say with certainty which outward signals helped the Good Thief recognize Jesus as Lord. But we do know that there was an inward change. The Holy Spirit prodded his heart! He was converted, not just by piecing together clues of simple observation. If that was the case, everyone would have accepted Christ as the Chosen One of God. Rather, the Spirit prompted his heart, and the Good Thief acknowledged the Good News!

Not all conversions are the same. Some people fully commit themselves to God even as they are living honorable lives. Joseph was called righteous. Mary was obedient. They were sinners, to be sure. But they did not share the outlaw past of the criminals on the cross. Some conversions are more dramatic, especially those who come to Christ in desperation like the Good Thief. For instance, Saul of Tarsus was a killer with bloodlust for the young Christian church. On the road to Damascus to persecute followers of the Way, Saul was stricken by a vision of Christ and converted on the spot. A short time later, with his name changed to Paul, he became a driving force in the early church.[35]

Many of the lifelong members of my church do not recognize a single moment of conversion. They grew up in the church faith and committed their heart to God at various stages of their lives. There were no drunken confessions or desperate cries from prison. Some converted at a young age and then recommitted in different seasons of life.

There is a common denominator in all conversions: brokenness. The Good Thief was spent. His body was broken, and his revolution had failed. He came to Christ as many do, with nothing to spare. The prodigal son returned only after he began to starve.[36] Zacchaeus was so despised by his community that he had to climb a tree![37] The converted were out of options. Their outward reality was a reflection of their inward brokenness. The Good Thief had nowhere to go. Instead of doubling down on his misery (like the Scoffer), he called out to Christ in humility.

The Good Thief lacked the typical criteria for salvation. He was never catechized or baptized. There was no articulation of the faith or recitation of church dogma. He never explained the gospel to anyone. The Good Thief did not receive any sacraments or have his name listed on a church roll. He just came to Jesus, as he was, in the moment. The Good Thief had just as much information as the man who was born blind in John 9. When Jesus healed him of his blindness, the religious leaders wanted to speculate about the theological ramifications. The man looked at them and gave a simple answer, "I was blind...but now I see."[38] All conversion is the same. We can dress it up in church clothes and a parade. But at its core, every conversion is like that of the Good Thief. We come empty-handed and receive paradise.

Jesus Receives the Sinner

When Jesus heard the confession of the Good Thief, he spoke to him in soft, gentle language. He did not always speak with soft words. Jesus used sharp rhetoric as he approached Calvary. One of his last sermons was a rebuke of the religious leaders in Jerusalem.[39] He derided the religious leaders for their hypocrisy. When he went into the city, he upended the Temple.[40] But to the Good Thief, who offered sincere remorse and recognition of Jesus as Lord, he spoke tenderly:

> *Truly I tell you, today you will be with me in Paradise.*[41]

"Truly I tell you": The Greek word is familiar to many: Ἀμήν, which translates "Amen."[42] The word connotes a trustworthy or proverbial saying. It was used by Jesus, especially in the parables explaining the Kingdom of God. Jesus garnered the attention of the Good Thief to help him hear that his words were divine. This was not a casual conversation. By opening with "Truly I tell you" (also translated "amen, amen"), Jesus signaled that a profound lesson would follow. The next words to come from Jesus's mouth would not be sunny optimism. Rather, they would be an important lesson about eternity.

We notice, too, that Jesus spoke directly to the Good Thief: "Truly I tell *you*" (emphasis mine). Jesus did not just preach to massive crowds. On numerous occasions, he conversed with individuals. The conversation with the Good Thief reminds us that Jesus speaks to us individually. Conversion is a personal experience. Our journey with him is unique. The old hymn is true: "He walks with me and he talks with me."[43] Jesus does not save the masses as a collective unit. We are each prompted by the Holy Spirit to convert as individuals. Jesus speaks to you; he speaks to me. In Galatians, Paul said:

> *I have been crucified with Christ and I no longer live, but Christ lives in me. The life I now live in the body, I live by faith in the Son of God, who loved me and gave himself for me.*[44]

"Today": The criminal is going to enjoy the reward of Christ "today." This word "sēmeron"(σήμερον) implies immediacy; it is properly translated as "now."[45] The long-awaited Kingdom of God is not a far-off ideal. The Good Thief sensed the victory of

Christ, and on that day, he would get to see it in full. Evil has had its hour on earth. Satan has been the "ruler of the air."[46] In eternity, just past death's door, the Good Thief was going to experience Jesus's victory over death and condemnation. As Charles Spurgeon said, "This man who was our Lord's last companion on earth [was his] first companion at the gates of paradise."[47]

"You will be with me": This is the promise of communion. For what purpose are we saved? To worship? For service? Certainly! But a benefit of our salvation that is often overlooked is our opportunity to commune with God in Jesus. We get to be "with" Jesus in a close, intimate relationship. Jesus said we should "abide in him."[48] In the Upper Room, John rested his head on the chest of Jesus as a sign of the connection we can enjoy in our relationship with him. From the cross, Jesus promised the Good Thief that his eternity would be in the presence of the Savior!

"In Paradise": This is a reference to the Garden of Eden, God's original intention for humanity. God created a place for humanity to dwell, a place of abundance and satisfaction. But sin wrecked the harmony of the garden and our relationship with God. When Adam and Eve ate the forbidden fruit, they were expelled from the garden, never to return.

To receive Christ is to regain entry into God's paradise. Heaven is a return to God's ideal for his creation. Sin entered the world through disobedience. Adam and Eve ate the fruit of a tree. In Revelation, there is a "tree of life" that is a symbol of the restored relationship with God.[49] On Calvary, Jesus hung on a tree as the bridge between fallen earth and perfect heaven. His tree represents the sin and brokenness of the world. Paradise was lost in Eden, and it will be restored in eternity. Jesus is the mediator, fully God and fully man, who offers us a way to God's original intention for us. The Good Thief would enjoy the paradise God designed in Eden.

The Good Thief made a simple plea to Jesus: "Remember me when you come into your kingdom." But Jesus promised something far greater than his request. Rather than just remembering him, Jesus offered him communion. Instead of a kingdom, which the Good Thief likely imagined as an improved version of the world, Jesus offered him paradise. In Christ, we are offered a life with God that far exceeds our imagination. In his letter to the Ephesians, Paul reminds us how God's provision is greater than our requests:

> *Now to him who is able to do immeasurably more than all we ask or imagine, according to his power that is at work within us, to him be glory in the church and in Christ Jesus throughout all generations, for ever and ever! Amen.*[50]

On Calvary, there were three crosses that held three captives. On one cross was the Scoffer, a guilty man who lived his last moments in misery. He was guilty of his crimes and made no sign of sorrow or remorse. The Scoffer remained in his guilt. On the second cross was the Good Thief, also a guilty man. Though we are not told of his crimes, we know he was guilty. He admitted as much. The Good Thief is so named because he admitted his guilt and made a crude but effective confession to Jesus. Though his body was still being punished by the state, his soul was now clean. He was saved. Unlike the Scoffer, this guilty man became innocent.

The third cross held our Savior, Jesus Christ. Though he was convicted of blasphemy, he was innocent. The charges were drummed up because he represented a threat to the established order. Jesus committed no crime and had no guilt. Yet there he was, condemned to die. While the Scoffer was a guilty man who remained in his guilt and the Good Thief was a guilty man who became innocent, Jesus was an innocent man who became guilty. He took on our sin, bearing the weight of our disobedience and sin. On Calvary, the guilty became innocent and the innocent became guilty; all so that we could receive forgiveness and enter into the paradise of God's design. By his death and resurrection, we are carriers of that great hope of eternal rest in Christ.

---

[1] Matthew 6:10
[2] 1 Peter 2:9-10
[3] 1 Corinthians 13:12
[4] Luke 23:43

[5] Darabont, Frank, Niki Marvin, Tim Robbins, Morgan Freeman, Bob Gunton, William Sadler, Clancy Brown, et al. 2004. *The Shawshank Redemption*. Burbank, CA: Warner Bros Pictures.

[6] Matthew 27:33

[7] Matthew 21:9, Mark 11:9

[8] Luke 9:46

[9] Isaiah 53:12

[10] Luke 22:37

[11] Mark 2:13-17

[12] Luke 7:39

[13] Luke 17:19

[14] James Strong, *Strong's Expanded Exhaustive Concordance of the Bible* (Nashville: Thomas Nelson, 2009), s.v. "léstés"

[15] Luke 23:39

[16] Luke 24:26

[17] Matthew 26:53

[18] Matthew 4:1-11

[19] Matthew 27:44

[20] Luke 23:40-41

[21] Luke 23:41b

[22] Luke 23:4

[23] Matthew 27:24

[24] Luke 23:42

[25] Luke 17:13; The demons also called him "Jesus" (see Luke 4:34). As he entered Jerusalem, an adoring crowd also called him by his proper name.

[26] James Martin, *Seven Last Words: An Invitation to a Deeper Friendship with Jesus*. Kindle Edition. (New York: HarperOne, 2015), 34.

[27] Mark 10:37

[28] Deuteronomy 7:9, Psalm 105:8

[29] Deuteronomy 5:6, 20:2

[30] Erwin W. Lutzer, *Cries from the Cross: A Journey into the Heart of Jesus*. (Chicago: Moody Publishers, 2015). Kindle Edition. 56.

[31] Warren W. Wiersbe, *The Cross of Jesus: What His Words from Calvary Mean for Us*. (Grand Rapids, MI: Baker Publishing, 1997). Kindle Edition. Loc 810.

[32] Isaiah 40:7

[33] Matthew 27:37

[34] Warren W. Wiersbe, *The Cross of Jesus: What His Words from Calvary Mean for Us*. (Grand Rapids: Baker Publishing Group, 1997). Kindle Edition. Loc 655.

[35] Acts 9:1-19

[36] Luke 15:17

[37] Luke 19:1-10

[38] John 9:25

[39] Matthew 23

[40] Matthew 21:12-17

[41] Luke 23:43

[42] James Strong, *Strong's Expanded Exhaustive Concordance of the Bible.* (Nashville: Thomas Nelson, 2009), s.v. "amen"

[43] Miles, Austin. Hymn: In the Garden

[44] Galatians 2:20

[45] James Strong, Strong's Expanded Exhaustive Concordance of the Bible (Nashville: Thomas Nelson, 2009), s.v. "sēmeron"

[46] Ephesians 2:2

[47] Erwin W. Lutzer, *Cries from the Cross: A Journey into the Heart of Jesus.* (Chicago: Moody Publishers, 2015). Kindle Edition. 52.

[48] John 15:4

[49] Revelation 2:7; 22:2, 14, 19

[50] Ephesians 3:20-21

Step Three - A New Community

"Woman, here is your son…here is your mother."
John 19:26-27

The third step in the journey toward Christian maturity is to engage in the life of the church. For many, church is an address. It is a place you go to worship. But the biblical definition of church is more broad and beautiful. The Greek word for church, ekklesia (ἐκκλησία), means "gathering."[1] The church, as defined by Scripture, is the gathering of believers for worship, fellowship, and service to others. Simple as that. When we hear the word "church," all sorts of images come to our mind: cathedrals, stained glass, preachers, pews, and so on. But the church is more than her symbols and structures. The church is the body of believers called together to reflect the glory of God. Christians are called to community because without one another we will not grow in Christ. Joining a local church is essential to a vibrant life with God.

Time for a confession: I was not initially impressed with this thing called "church." In my formative years, I did not see the value in the weekly ritual. I was raised in a formal and traditional Quaker congregation. It was about as exciting as you would imagine a formal and traditional Quaker congregation. It was like the Mennonites without all the pizzazz. From my view on the back pew (or bench, as Quakers call them), I sat behind a sea of gray hair. Church was the longest hour of my week. I played tic-tac-toe, drew portraits of the back of people's heads, colored the bulletin…anything to pass the time. The seconds never moved slower. My grandfather was the pastor of that church for thirty-six years, through my early teenage years. I am told he was a very thoughtful minister and a great communicator. I would not know. I spent my years in church with my head down wishing the minutes away.

But I am forever grateful for those years on the back bench of Springfield Friends Meeting in High Point, North Carolina. Though I did not recognize it at the time, something very important was forming deep within my spirit. Seeds of the gospel were planted and nurtured. I was being shaped and molded by a community of faith that would celebrate my faith and send me into the world to share the gospel.

I assumed the modest, meek congregation of seniors met out of pure routine; why else would anyone sit through church? But it was a tight-knit community. They cared for one another, encouraged each other in the faith, and supported youth ministries that would shape my identity in Christ. Some of my earliest memories are of a tired and haggled Sunday school teacher trying to teach us the gospel stories while we ran around the room. My first recollection of the Christmas story is when I was cast in a starring role (Sheep #2) in the nativity play.

At vacation Bible school, I sang the songs and played the games. At Quaker Kids Club, I remember sitting on the Kool-Aid-stained carpet while my grandmother faithfully (and patiently) taught us the Lord's Prayer. In senior high youth group, my eyes were opened to the meaning of the Scriptures, and I learned important doctrines of the faith. At church I was encouraged, corrected, exhorted, and nurtured. All the while, I was thinking it was just another activity in my life. Little did I know, the church was inculcating the gospel in my life. With each prayer, worship hour, potluck, Bible lesson and activity, the Word was being knit into my life.

The seed that was planted in the church nursery and nurtured in youth group eventually took root. At seventeen years old, I heard a gospel message that was, all at once, brand new and yet familiar. I accepted Jesus Christ as my Savior and was born again. It was one decision, but it was the culmination of a lifetime of Christian nurture.

On its face, church can look like an immensely dull place, in utter contrast with the blinding tempo of the world. We use odd symbols, have our own vocabulary ("the bulletins are in the narthex"), and teach a message at odds with an increasingly secular society. The church is messy, too. I do not want to mythologize the congregation of my upbringing. It had plenty of sinners, just like every other church in Christendom. There were bullies, liars, and hypocrites who sat neatly beside the saints. Through it all, the message of grace and reconciliation remains. It is a glorious mess. This is the church, the body of Christ.

Flawed and disheveled, the church is still one of the ways God reveals himself to the world. The church is the carrier of the gospel message from one generation to the next. It is intended to be an image of the Church in Heaven: at worship, fellowship, and the constant pursuit of divine justice. Those ideals are never met, not on this side of heaven, anyway.

As we will see, this third word from Jesus is a call to community. Though he directly addresses family ties with this statement, there is a deeper call for us to be part of the family of God. This leads us to *Step Three: A New Community.* The church is not just beneficial to the life of the believer. It is essential. It is impossible to grow to your potential in faith without a Christian community.

Those who were once isolated from God are brought close to him in Christ. Further still, we are brought close to one another in the church. Religion is always a social affair. We need each other in order to grow and mature in the faith.

There is a popular, almost ingrained, cultural sentiment that says we can be spiritual without a faith community. Many believe that spirituality is an individual experience. As if we have a beautiful soul that flowers on its own. They think the church just adds rules and formality to an otherwise flourishing spiritual life. Indeed, every person has a spiritual nature. We all instinctively and intuitively tap into our inward spiritual sense of the divine. That is because we are all created in the image of God. But spirituality without community eventually runs dry. With no community of faith or healthy boundaries for the spiritual life, we end up navel gazing. People may find some comfort in self-evaluation, but those waters are not deep. All shallows are clear.

One of the great ironies of our inter-connected age is that we are increasingly lonely. Social media has given us a platform by which we can broadcast our thoughts to the world at a moment's notice. In a matter of seconds, we can tell the entire world our political passions or what we had for dessert. We can keep up with our friends and spy on enemies. On the surface, it would seem we have found the cure for loneliness. After all, the internet has made the world a very small place.

Yet loneliness and isolation are on the rise. A recent study revealed that social media use has a direct correlation to personal loneliness.[2] There is simply no "platform" that can duplicate actual one-on-one interaction. We need to be with people. There was a time, not too long ago, when being with other people was a given. People needed their communities. They knew their neighbors. But today you can point and click and have your necessities delivered to your door. Instead of chatting with neighbors, you can "like" Facebook pictures. However, the longing for genuine community is not satisfied by online social networks. We are created by a God who designed us to be with others.

Jesus invites us to his community, the church. The cross is a stake pointing up and a beam extending outward. We are called to a heavenward relationship with God and holy relationships with one another. In this simple statement from the cross, addressed to his grieving mother, we hear the call to join the body of Christ. Let's examine this word from Jesus and hear how he calls his followers into the life of the church.

Son and Mother

Jesus's third word from the cross is to his mother. Luke's gospel contains the first two words from the cross. We now turn to John's gospel to hear the next. By this time, Jesus has been on the cross all morning. The minutes have turned to hours. At the first word, Jesus looked up to address God his Father in prayer. For the second word, he looked over and addressed a penitent criminal. Next, he looked down to his grieving mother and spoke.

This is a gruesome scene. As Jesus hung upon the cross, his blood dripping beneath, the soldiers were arguing over his last possession. Four soldiers were dividing Jesus's clothes among them. In those days, people wore five pieces of clothing.[3] The four soldiers each took one; now there was one piece over which to haggle. They treated the dying man's final belonging like it was the last piece of chicken on the dinner table. Rather than argue and fight, they cast lots. Perhaps they each wanted a souvenir or some extra cloth to barter. Either way, it was a crass and cynical moment. It is another glimpse into the carnal and fickle desires of humanity. Our world is full of injustice and violence, much of which is well within our purview. It's easier to haggle over the garments than look to the mess that sin has wrought.

It is at this moment, as the soldiers were bartering for his last possession, that Jesus spoke to his mother. It raises the question, "Why now?" Certainly Mary was present during the entire ordeal. She had not left his side. A caring mother would cross an ocean to ease the suffering of her child. Why did Jesus use this moment to speak to her?

The garment is a clue. Some have speculated that this garment was a gift from Mary to Jesus. She would have made it herself and gifted it to him. It was common practice in ancient days. Perhaps Jesus saw the anguish on his mother's face at the callous removal and barter of her gift to him. It would have been another painful strike to the heart of a mother who had already suffered so much. Mary bore and labored the Christ-child into the world and held her naked and screaming infant. She "wrapped him in swaddling clothes" and held him close.[4] Perhaps Jesus spoke to her because her grief was piercing as she watched her gift to him bartered away by callous soldiers.

Now the garments had been ripped away. He was naked and bleeding with tears rolling to his chin. She wanted to cover him again and ease the cries of her child. But she could not. She was helpless. The religious leaders won the day. The state had served the sentence. Everything he once had was now gone, even his last garment. It is hard to comprehend Mary's anguish.

This scene is more than just a moment in history. It is a ghastly display of how far the world had veered from God's original intention. Before the fall into sin in the Garden of Eden, Adam and Eve were sinless and unashamed. They were naked and exposed, and yet there was no embarrassment. After the fall, they saw each other naked and wanted to hide. After Eden, nudity equates to shame and vulnerability. On the cross, Jesus was stripped and nude for everyone to see. Mary could only watch in horror as her son faced the wrath of a fallen world.

In the hours of pain, it is natural to turn our thoughts inward. But even in the horror of the cross, Jesus turned his attention to the concerns of others. As he looked upon his mother's grief, he sought to both console her and assure she would be protected in his absence. Throughout his ministry, Jesus taught his followers to put the concerns of others before themselves: "Do to others as you would have them do to you."[5] In the third word, Jesus practiced what he preached:

> *When Jesus saw his mother there, and the disciple whom he loved standing nearby, he said to her, "Woman, here is your son."*[6]

"Woman": Why did Jesus call her "woman" instead of "mother"? It appears as a slight until we understand the context. Jesus never referred to Mary as mother. For example, early in the gospel of John, while attending a wedding in Cana, the host of the party ran out of wine. When Mary brought the concern to Jesus, he said, "Woman, why do you involve me?"[7]

Jesus had a special role in the world, one that disconnected him from typical family relationships. Even though Jesus was unique, he still followed the domestic customs of his day. He was a product of his home. Jesus enjoyed the nurture of Mary and Joseph. At the third word, Jesus was fulfilling his role as a firstborn son to care for the well-being of his mother in her old age. Most scholars believe that Joseph died well before Jesus began his ministry. After the birth narrative, Joseph is never mentioned again. With his earthly father gone and Jesus enduring his last moments on earth, he knew he would not be there to tend to her needs in old age. So he committed her to the care of a trusted friend.

However, we see that Jesus's bond with his earthly family was superseded by his relationship with God the Father. When Jesus called his mother "woman," it signified the genuinely unique relationship between Jesus and Mary. There has never been, nor will there ever be, a relationship as peculiar as Jesus and Mary's. Every other parent seeks to nurture and care for the well-being of her children that they might thrive. But Jesus's vocation in the world, the purpose of his life, was to die on the cross for the sins of the world. That includes Mary's sins. On the cross, Jesus was no longer just Mary's son, he was her Savior.

Mary sang of this salvation before Jesus was born. In the Magnificat, she praised God who was "my Savior."[8] She was singing of the child in her womb. Mary recognized the uniqueness of Jesus early in his life. When they had to return to Jerusalem after the Passover pilgrimage, they found Jesus in the Temple confounding the rabbis with his wisdom.[9] Mary "treasured these things in her heart."[10] From the time she committed in obedience to bear him in her womb to the cross, Mary knew her son had a special role in God's plan.

"Here is your son": The Greek word for "here is" (ide, ἴδε) implies urgency. Several translations render the word as "behold," which better captures the tone. To "behold" (ide) something is to fix your eyes and ponder. You look at a stop sign, but you behold a sunset. We may look at people crossing the street, but we behold a parade. You look at a stranger, but you behold a newborn baby.

Jesus was asking his mother to do something very important. She was to behold the disciple John as her new family. The familial ties that she had with Jesus were no more. She was now to be welcomed into a new family, represented by John. Jesus honored the Law and was obeying the fifth commandment to "honor [his] father and mother."[11] Because he would be absent, Jesus was making sure his mother would be cared for. Scripture tells us that John would "welcome her into his home"[12] and thus care for her in years to come. Mary's fear of isolation could be calmed. She would not be alone; she would be part of a larger family.

Why didn't Jesus ask a blood relative to care for Mary? Mary had sons and nephews among the disciples, and it is Jewish custom for a relative to care for a widow. But Jesus signaled that the care for his mother would come from the church. This signals that those who confess their faith in Christ would form a body that would care for the vulnerable.

Jesus spoke about his relationship with his immediate family. While preaching, teaching, and healing in a small town, Jesus was told his family was waiting on him outside. Jesus replied:

> *'Who are my mother and my brothers?'*
> *Then he looked at those seated in a circle*
> *around him and said,*
> *'Here are my mother and my brothers!*
> *Whoever does God's will is my brother and*
> *sister and mother.'*[13]

Those who are in submission to him and follow his commands are his family. Again, Jesus had a unique relationship with his family, comes with a new family. We are welcomed into a mystical communion with other believers. It is hard for us to imagine today, as we live such insulated lives. But just a few generations ago, the world was a collection of smaller, tight-knit communities. The church was to be the model and emblem of God's desire for community. We read about the tight-knit Christian community in the book of Acts:

> *All the believers were together and had everything in common. They sold property and possessions to give to anyone who had need. Every day they continued to meet together in the temple courts. They broke bread in their homes and ate together with glad and sincere hearts, praising God and enjoying the favor of all the people. And the Lord added to their number daily those who were being saved.*[14]

The church is not an address or a set of programs. We do not join a church to gain status. The confession of Jesus Christ as Savior immediately grafts us into the body of Christ, where we learn from our church family how to become more Christ-like.

My wife and I were privileged to witness an adoption ceremony at a local courthouse. Some friends of ours had fostered two girls for several months, carefully navigated the adoption bureaucracy, and were ready to call these children their own. With the court's blessing and in the presence of their friends, the judge read a carefully prepared statement about the requirements and responsibilities of adoption. At the conclusion of the statement and with a final affirmation from the parents, the judge hit the desk with a gavel, and adoption was final. In that moment, two girls who were once deprived of a decent upbringing and home life were welcomed into a "forever family." At the judge's pronouncement, the kids received new birth certificates, new identities, and new names. They were once isolated and vulnerable, but now they had a family.

The story rings true for Christians. In sin, we are isolated and adrift. When we come into Christ, we receive a new birth, a reformed identity, and a new family we call church. Though they were not blood relatives, Jesus united John and Mary with a spiritual bond. Their unity is a beautiful symbol for everyone who confesses Christ as Lord and is welcomed into his church.

Grace between the Lines

In the second part of the statement, Jesus uses the formal term "son" to describe John. This is an odd distinction because Jesus was roughly the same age as John. To be a son was to be in a lower status among the family. It meant you were in submission to a father. Add to that, Jesus was hardly in a physical position to deem anyone a "son" or other subservient position. A crucified person is obviously not in a place of high status; yet even in that moment, Jesus was reckoning himself as authoritative. He is the head of the church. Later in the New Testament, this image would be reinforced over and again.[15] In referring to John as son, Jesus was claiming himself as the head of the church, where he will reign for all eternity.

It must have been reassuring for John to hear Jesus call him a "son." That is language reserved for family. John was restored to discipleship under Jesus. Earlier in the gospel story, John rested his head on the chest of Jesus and proclaimed devotion to him.[16] After the arrest in the Garden of Gethsemane, all of the disciples betrayed Jesus, including John. But John returned to witness the crucifixion.

Jesus could have lashed out at this betrayal. Anyone who has ever been betrayed knows the depths of pain and righteous anger that swells within. No one would have blamed Jesus for cursing his supposed "friend." But Jesus restored John. He acted in alignment with his initial prayer for forgiveness for his enemies. Even from the pain of the cross, Jesus welcomed the sinner.

The gospel describes John as "the disciple whom Jesus loved."[17] This reference says more about Jesus than it does about John. The disciple was not boasting of his privileged status among the disciples. Rather, to be called "the disciple who Jesus loved" highlights the incredible grace of Jesus, who accepted the contrition and repentance of one who had betrayed him in his hour of need.

Those who have fallen away from the faith are invited to return to him. How many of us have passionately proclaimed Jesus as Lord of our life only to spend whole seasons of our life drifting from him? The good news is that we can return to Christ in sincere repentance. When we return to him, we are welcomed as a "son" or "daughter" to the one who gained our restoration on Calvary.

"Here is your mother": After Jesus united John and Mary, he spoke to John. Once again, the urgent (ide, ἴδε) is used. Jesus insisted that John "behold" Mary, as she was his new family member. He was to have his eyes open to Mary.

Let's pause for a moment and consider what John would have "beheld" when he turned his eyes to Mary. When we imagine Mary, our minds conjure a picture of simple beauty. Some of the most beautiful paintings and sculptures are of Mary, usually in gentle repose, gazing at her Christ-child. We are encouraged to think of Mary in mythological terms, as if she never felt pain or grieved.

But on the hill called the Skull,[18] I cannot imagine Mary was a portrait of grace and strength. I have sat with grieving mothers. Their pain is hell: weeping, gnashing, and bellowing sorrow. A mother's heart is a deep well of love. Their instinct is to protect. When their child suffers, there is no deeper misery. In this moment, as she watched her son die a criminal's death, Mary was not the gentle and meek wife of a humble carpenter. She was a wretched mess.

John was looking at a broken and vulnerable soul. Mary had no husband, her relatives were absent, and her son's only possession (the garment) was being sold off like cheap fare. She was at a complete loss. She had nothing to offer and no place to go.

Jesus told John to "behold" Mary. That is, to see her in all of her pain and anguish. Most of us do not like to look at the vulnerable or address the sin that has caused so much damage. Like the soldiers haggling over Jesus's last garment, we like to keep our heads down and focus on the stuff we want. But the call of the Christian is to "behold" the pain of the world. The church cannot neglect those who suffer. The third word from the cross is a call to the church to behold the pain of the world.

Before Jesus was arrested and sentenced, he spent time in Bethany, a small town just outside Jerusalem.[19] There he dined at the home of a Pharisee named Simon. While enjoying the meal, a woman with a reputation for low virtue (to put it politely) barged in and groveled at the feet of Jesus. She recognized him as a prophet of God and sensed her need to repent of her sin. Overwhelmed by her sin and aware of his glory, she wept at Jesus's feet, using her tear-drenched hair to wipe his feet.

What was Simon to do? What would you do? The Pharisee

used the occasion to both shame the woman and test Jesus. If this man were a prophet, he said, he would certainly not allow this sinful woman to touch him!

It was a conundrum for Jesus. He was trapped! If he said she was not a sinner, Jesus would be lying about his authority. But if she was allowed to touch him, then he was not really a prophet. It was a "gotcha" moment for Simon.

But Jesus turned the quagmire on its head. Simon was concerned about the religious decorum. But Jesus was concerned about the suffering, penitent woman. In a stunning and poignant statement, Jesus asked the devout Pharisee:

Do you see this woman?[20]

To put it another way, "Through all of the religious score-keeping and theological banter, can you see the hurting person?"

Jesus went on to tell a parable about honest sinners who are gracious in their repentance. It is the sick who need a doctor, not the "righteous" who are certain of their good spiritual health. Simon had his eyes open to the correct rituals, but he was blind to the actual needs of a hurting person.

John was faced with the same challenge. He must behold the vulnerable Mary. He must see the grieving widow. Here was a person with no home, no future, and no prospects. The church is called to have its eyes open to the pain and injustice of the world, to behold the hell on earth that sin has wrought.

Many Christians do not want to "behold" any such thing. It is much easier to keep our eyes lifted to God in worship. When we look around in church, we want to see people who look and act just like us. We put on the nice clothes, sit in the same pews, shake the same hands, and behold Sunday morning niceties. That may be enjoyable, but it is not the call of the church. The body of Christ is to behold the hurting, hungry, and grieving. James put it bluntly:

> *Religion that God our Father accepts as pure and faultless is this: to look after orphans and widows in their distress and to keep oneself from being polluted by the world.*[21]

Step Three - A New Community

Our church began a local outreach ministry with the intention of seeing the actual needs in our community. We ventured into poverty-stricken areas of our rural community. These pockets of poverty are just a few miles from our beautiful church campus. Some of our neighbors live in campers, run-down trailers, and dilapidated homes. It did not take very long before our eyes were open to the brokenness within our community. Drug abuse, domestic violence, food insecurity, and isolation were right next door. For too long, we had refused to see the vulnerable who were right beside us.

We have formed several good relationships through our local outreach ministry. There are fine people who live in that community. Just as you cannot judge a book by its cover, so too you cannot judge a person by where they live. Many are kind, decent, hardworking people. Some have come to know Christ as Savior and have begun to share the good news with their neighbors!

Still, many in our community do not live well. Do we really want to see that? Do we want to be engaged with our neighbors who do not live, look, dress, and behave as we do? If we are to follow Jesus, we must lay our eyes on the actual conditions of our community. It is not pretty, and there are no easy fixes. But as Jesus told John to behold the hurting, grieving widow, so we are supposed to see the sorrow and pain all around. Only when we behold the pain can we initiate the "kingdom come" and do the gospel work to which we are called.

Thankfully, our church continues the good work to the hurting and vulnerable in our community. We began a community meal as an effort to help otherwise isolated people rub elbows. Great friendships have emerged. We started a faith-based drug recovery program to help people in their fight against addiction. It is messy, and there are plenty of setbacks. But each time we open the doors and proclaim the gospel of Christ, we are fighting against the tide of grief, sorrow, and pain so prevalent in our rural community.

John was obedient and took Mary into his home and cared for her.[22] After the death and burial of Jesus, some women were visiting the tomb on the third day. When they found the stone rolled away and the tomb empty, they rushed to the disciples and announced the good news. With the disciples, Mary received the first sermon, "He is risen!" There is an image of the church: John, the restored sinner, with Mary, the recipient of care and nurture, hearing the good news of the risen Christ!

A Fire on the Earth

There is an old story of a pastor who went to visit one of his church members who lived on a prairie. The church member had not been to worship in a long time, and it concerned the pastor. When the pastor arrived, the two visited in front of the fire. The church member explained that he did not need to go to church because he could just pray and worship on his own. The pastor listened intently, waiting for his turn to speak. After the church member said his piece, the pastor quietly lifted a fork from beside the fireplace and drew out a flaming, red coal. He placed it gently on the brick. They both watched silently as the red coal turned black and cold. Neither said a word, but the point was made.

In order to grow in spiritual maturity, Christians need to be with one another. Jesus said, "I have come to bring fire on the earth, and how I wish it were already kindled [among you]!"[23] Christians are the "brush" by which the Spirit of God burns. Just as a single match has a small flame that quickly burns out, so too a believer who is not in community. But a bundle of kindling burns bright and hot! The gathered church body welcomes the fire of the Holy Spirit and, bound together like kindling, the light burns brightly among the faithful.

Christians need each other to grow in faith in Christ. The unification of John and Mary is a symbol for the church to be in constant community and fellowship. Again, we are not going to reach spiritual maturity without a body of believers to engage, correct, and encourage us. Together, we become the hands and feet of God in the world, enacting his mercy and justice in a fallen world.

---

[1] James Strong, *Strong's Expanded Exhaustive Concordance of the Bible* (Nashville: Thomas Nelson, 2009), s.v. "ekklésia"

[2] https://www.psychologytoday.com/us/blog/modern- mentality/201810/is-social-media-making-you-lonely

[3] Erwin W. Lutzer, *Cries from the Cross: A Journey into the Heart of Jesus* (Chicago: Moody Publishers, 2015), Kindle Edition. 60.

[4] Luke 2:7
[5] Luke 6:31
[6] John 19:26-27
[7] John 2:4
[8] Luke 1:46-55
[9] Luke 2:41-52
[10] Luke 2:51
[11] Exodus 20:12
[12] John 19:27
[13] Mark 3:31-35
[14] Acts 2:42-46
[15] Romans 12:5, 1 Corinthians 12:12–27, Ephesians 3:6, 5:23, Colossians 1:18, 24
[16] John 13:23
[17] John 20:2
[18] Matthew 27:33
[19] Luke 7:36-50
[20] Luke 7:44
[21] James 1:27
[22] John 19:27
[23] Luke 12:49

Step Four - Wrestling with God

"My God, my God, why have you forsaken me?"
Mark 15:34; Matthew 27:46

The dentist broke the news to us: our oldest daughter had to have a few teeth removed. At eleven years old, her mouth was crowded, and some teeth had to come out to make room. My wife and I tried to take the news in stride. We can handle this, no big deal. A shot, a pull, and yank, and we would be done. Then the other shoe dropped: Lucy was going to need oral surgery. Full on, knocked out, day-long-ordeal surgery. Of course, Emily and I were nervous about the whole thing, but we tried not to let it show.

When the big day finally came, Lucy marched from the waiting room into the care of the oral surgeon. Our little girl was growing up. She was a champ. Everything went as expected; no complications with the surgery.

When the nurses called us back to see Lucy, we found her with a large bandage wrapped around her head and tears streaming down her swollen cheeks. It was a tough day. As she recovered, Lucy told us that she had been really nervous about the surgery. We were all trying to be brave for the benefit of each other.

I asked her how, if she was so nervous, she could go with doctors who she did not know, into a room separate from us.

With child-like confidence, she looked up and said, "I knew you were out there."

Lucy was nervous, separated, and scared, but she knew we would be together again soon.

The fourth word from the cross is a cry of separation. Jesus called out:

My God, my God, why have you forsaken me?[1]

This word offers a glimpse into the pain of separation. Jesus was apart from his Father. He needed help, and yet God was silent. But this was not a last gasp of desperation. Jesus was not angry and losing his faith. There was hope, even in the cry for help. Reunion with the Father and redemption for the world would soon follow.

This mysterious and perplexing statement represents another step in Christian maturity: *Step Four: Wrestling with God*. In order to grow in Christ, there must be periods of tension with God. Our relationship with God is not a romance; it is a marriage. We grow closer to God through every season of our life. Believers are drawn close to him after we walk through valleys of doubt and anxiousness.

It is normal to trust God in the throes of worship, when hearts are focused on his presence. We adore God in his church and in the company of believers. But the Christian journey is not all Sunday worship and small-group Bible studies. Our life is full of disappointment and grief. We call to God in those desperate hours, but hear no reply. Where is God? Why is he silent? Has he abandoned us? Part of spiritual growth is trusting in God when he seems distant. Do we trust God in our hours of desperation? Can we cry and lament to God, knowing he will act in his time? Christian maturity requires we grapple with God, that we lift our hearts and trust, even when our lips say, "My God, my God, why have you forsaken me?"

A healthy, vibrant, and maturing spiritual life must include a friction with God. When a young couple falls in love, they are enamored with each other. It is puppy love. The other can do no wrong. But this is not real love; it is infatuation. Mature love emerges when the couple begins to see each other in a true light. They disagree and quarrel. If they love each other, they will stay and reconcile their differences, eventually learning to love the quirks of the other. Otherwise, it is on to the next romance.

Many Christians never move beyond their infatuation with God. The first three steps of the journey are exciting: We are forgiven by God and enjoy a blissful rebirth (step one). The teachings of Jesus show us how to live as citizens of a new kingdom (step two). No longer isolated, we join a church and engage in worship and community (step three). The first stages are (relatively) painless, even joyful!

But some never move beyond spiritual adolescence. For years, even decades, well-meaning Christians enjoy preaching, teaching, and church community while never daring to lean into the deeper mysteries of God. They are stuck in spiritual neutral. Just as standing water becomes murky, people who stop pursuing God become complacent. Bitterness and resentment begin to surface. It is possible to hear the Word of God, sing the songs of worship, learn the doctrine, and join the fellowship, all while rejecting a deeper life with God.

We need to wrestle with God. We need to trust when he is silent. Faith requires that we trust when we feel abandoned. Spiritual growth occurs when we delve into the mysterious life of God. Otherwise, the Christian is going on a constant search for another sensation, a fickle feeling of transcendence. Every pastor I know has heard, "I'm just not getting fed at church anymore," or "The church doesn't feel like it used to." Off they go, to the next church and the next, chasing a sensation. The most discontent Christians are those who have orbited the faith for years but have never truly grappled with God. They love God, but not enough to ask "why?"

It is here, at the fourth word, that we come to a crossroad. This is the halfway point in the words of the cross; a long way from the initial forgiveness and still at a distance from the rest our hearts desire. Either we are going to grapple with God and move toward a deeper, more intimate relationship with him or continue as babes in the faith.

Can we have faith during those moments of crisis? Can we call out to God in our agony and even voice our frustration, while still believing in his providential plan? These are some of the challenges posed by the fourth word from the cross. This is not the Sunday-school or bumper-sticker God, who solves all our problems and wraps the answer in a nice, tidy package. Here we are confronted with a God who leaves us to suffer and allows the evil forces of the world to temporarily succeed. Can we persist in faith even when the God we proclaim is seemingly absent? This is not for the faint of heart.

The Fourth Word

The fourth word is the most puzzling of the seven. There are no easy answers. These words of abandonment and separation, the only of their kind in the ministry of Jesus.

This word defies our expectations. We can accept the fact that Jesus would forgive his enemies (first word) and welcome a repentant sinner into heaven (second word). Would Jesus care for his mother (third word)? Of course! Those words fit our image of a gracious Lord. That is a Jesus we can enjoy and relate.

But what do we make of a Savior who says: *My God, my God...why have you forsaken me?*

Does this mean that Jesus was abandoned by God? Isn't Jesus supposed to be God? Doesn't he have a perfect connection with God the Father? Does God abandon people? So many questions arise from this profound statement.

To be sure, we will never fully understand the depth of meaning in this fourth word. Faith in God sometimes means we lean into the mystery with assurance that some things are beyond our knowledge. This word calls us to lean into a healthy tension with God. His ways are profound and mysterious. Sometimes he speaks with clarity and offers a well-lit path. Other times, God is silent. There are moments when we feel we need God to act or speak, and there is nothing. It is an agonizing stillness. In the push and pull, we learn to trust him in all seasons.

Darkness

Before we parse each word, let's look at the setting and some of the events surrounding this fourth statement.

This fourth word is the only one that we are told the time of the day it happened. The day began at 6 a.m., and Jesus was crucified at 9 a.m. His body hung on the cross for six long hours. The night before, Jesus told his enemies that "darkness" would reign, but only in this "hour."[2] At noon, the prophecy was fulfilled:

> *From noon until three in the afternoon*
> *darkness came over all the land.*[3]

The darkness is a powerful image. The Light of the world was shrouded in darkness. John's gospel tells us of the power of Light: Darkness has not understood it.[4] Light always wins over darkness. But at the cross, the Light of the world was extinguished.

Many have speculated about the cause of this darkness. The gospel of Luke alludes to a solar eclipse as the cause.[5] Perhaps it was a sand storm or thick rain clouds that caused the sunlight to cease. Whatever the cause, the darkness over Calvary was more than a physical manifestation. This darkness was more than the absence of light.

Throughout Scripture, darkness equates to chaos, death, and judgment. Before creation, the world was absent of light, and darkness abounded. Darkness represents chaos and the disorder that prevails in the absence of God's perfect order.

In Exodus, a plague of darkness was one of the ten plagues cast upon the Egyptians. The captors could not see their hands in front of their faces! God used darkness as judgment.[6] The absence of light was a form of punishment on those who oppressed God's people. At the cross, darkness was a poignant symbol that the enemies of God were bringing about another plague upon themselves.

Jesus contrasted light and darkness throughout his ministry. He proclaimed himself as "the Light of the world"[7] and his followers would be a well-lit "town on a hill" that cannot be hidden.[8] In the parables of Jesus, light was often a central image. A woman who lost a valuable coin turned on all the lights so she could find what was missing.[9] In darkness, thieves break in and steal,[10] the sheep are in danger,[11] and the unwise virgins are left out of the banquet.[12] In describing the worst judgment, those who are eternally separated from the Kingdom of God, Jesus referred to "outer darkness."[13]

But thankfully, darkness is not the end of the story. Just as the darkness of pre-creation was overcome by the light, so too the emptiness of death is overcome by Easter. Those walking in darkness have seen a great light.[14] The resurrection was the moment when light sprang forth to defeat our greatest, and darkest, enemy: death.

George Fox, the progenitor of the Quaker movement, spoke frequently of Jesus as the Light. When he preached in seventeenth-century England, he believed the state church to be an over-formalized, dry, and dark affair. In the presence of the Holy Spirit, Fox envisioned the great Light of God in Christ overcoming all darkness:

> *I saw also that there was an ocean of darkness and death, but an infinite ocean of light and love, which flowed over the ocean of darkness.*[15]

On Calvary, an "ocean of darkness" came over the land. Jesus was separated from his father, sin was upon him, and Satan had declared a victory. But the darkness of Friday was overcome by the Light of Sunday. Christ arose victorious, and the unending Light of God overcame all darkness. At the death of Jesus, the curtain in the Temple that separated the people from the holy of holies was torn from top to bottom.16 The tear came from the top down to signify God's initiative. The holiness of God was manifest in Jesus Christ. The Temple worship, which served as the vehicle for worship and sacrifice, was now obsolete. Jesus was the perfect sacrifice, and the world could know God through him.

"My God, my God": Jesus cried out in a foreign tongue:

> *'Eli, Eli lama sabachthani!' (which means 'My God, my God, why have you forsaken me?')*17

Like most people in ancient Israel, Jesus spoke Aramaic. It was the language of the common people. Israel has always been a by-way, criss-crossed by world powers. Empires occupied the promised land, bringing their languages and cultures with them. People spoke multiple languages based on their context. Latin was the language of the rulers; Greek was used in the marketplace, Aramaic on the street, and Hebrew in the Temple. Jesus's cry in Aramaic was intentional. There were no more formalities. This was a primitive cry from a man who had been reduced by the cross.

Thus far on the cross, Jesus had addressed his enemies, a sinner, and the saints. These represent the whole of humanity. But now Jesus turned his voice to God. In the fourth word, Jesus addressed God in a less personal way. Up to this moment, Jesus had enjoyed a unique and intimate connection with God.

As noted in previous chapters, Jesus referred to God as "Father" throughout his ministry. His relationship with God the Father was familial and personal. By living in perfect obedience and inextricable connection, Jesus rightly proclaimed: "I and the Father are one." The close connection Jesus had with the Father was one of the reasons he was so despised by the religious rulers. In their stiff obedience, they could not imagine an intimacy with God the rule-giver. Jesus defied those assumptions.

God is a gracious, loving Father. In speaking of his provision, Jesus said: When a child asks for bread, does his father give him a stone?[18] God is family, a father who provides and loves dearly. He cares for us more than the birds of the air and flowers of the field.[19] Jesus enjoyed constant communion with him and taught his followers to know God as a father.

This is why the cry of Jesus is so heartbreaking. We read that Jesus "cried out," which is translated "shout up" (ἀνεβόησεν).[20] Jesus called out to "my God, my God," which is much less personal. The dual cry ("my God, my God") implies a heightened sense of loss. "Is he listening? How many times do I need to call out?" The familiarity that Jesus once felt with the Father was now gone.

This is the darkest moment in the passion story. Jesus had never been abandoned by the Father. Everyone else had let him down. The disciples had betrayed him, the courts were unjust, and his physical body was wearing down. But just moments before, Jesus had conjured the strength to cry out, "Father! Forgive them!" He had referenced the paradise that God the Father promises his faithful children. Now, there was a disconnect. There was silence. Where was the Father who always promised to care and provide?

The feeling of forsakenness is a common experience among the faithful. In every meaningful journey with the Lord, there is a time of silence from God. This difficult experience should be a time of growth and maturity. God forms his people, not in times of abundance, but in the wilderness. Can you trust God when he is silent? Can you believe when you feel forsaken? This is a central question of faith. Anyone can believe when they "feel" and see the presence of God. But as Jesus said, "Blessed are those who believe and have not seen."[21]

Some letters of Mother Teresa were published after her death. She wrote to a close friend that she felt abandoned by God. She wondered if she even believed in God. The absence of his presence began to take a toll, and she had moments of despair and confusion. Perhaps she said to herself, "My God, why have you forsaken me?"

Does this mean Mother Teresa lost her faith and disavowed God? Certainly not. She would later write:

> *In the darkness... Lord, my God, who am I that You should forsake me?... I call, I cling, I want, and there is no one to answer... Where I try to raise my thoughts to heaven, there is such convicting emptiness that those very thoughts return like sharp knives and hurt my very soul... I am told God lives in me—and yet the reality of darkness and coldness and emptiness is so great that nothing touches my soul.*[22]

Experiencing a distance from God, which is often described as forsakenness, is not the exception in the maturing Christian life. It is the rule. In the fourth word from the cross, we are reminded that the path to peace with God must include a time of distance and disillusionment.

Psalm 22

The cry, "My God, my God, why have you forsaken me?" would have been familiar to the Jews in Jesus's day. Like most of Jesus's teachings, the words have origin in the Old Testament. Centuries before, David wrote:

> *My God, my God, why have you forsaken me? Why are you so far from saving me, so far from my cries of anguish?*
> *My God, I cry out by day, but you do not answer, by night, but I find no rest.*[23]

The psalm describes the pain of the forsaken, a divine foreshadowing of Calvary's torment. Warren Wiersbe notes the similarities between the 22nd Psalm and Calvary:

> *David was inspired by the Holy Spirit to write about the sufferings of our Lord on the cross. David described the darkness and light at Calvary (v. 2); the mockery of the unbelieving crowd (vv. 6–8); the physical*

> *suffering of the Savior, including the piercing of his hands and feet (vv. 14–16); the humiliation and shame he endured (v. 17); the gambling for his garments (v. 18); and the seeming hopelessness of the situation (vv. 19–21).*[24]

The psalm begins in agony (my God, my God, why have you forsaken me?), but it ends in glory. The suffering need not despair:

> *I will declare your name to my people;*
> *in the assembly I will praise you.*
> *You who fear the Lord, praise him!*
> *All you descendants of Jacob, honor him!*
> *Revere him, all you descendants of Israel!*
> *For he has not despised or scorned the*
> *suffering of the afflicted one;*
> *he has not hidden his face from him*
> *but has listened to his cry for help.*[25]

Jesus called out to God in desperation, quoting the first verses of this psalm. But he knew how the psalm ends. It is the same way the gospel story ends: with victory over death. Jesus endured the forsakenness of the cross and called out to God with the certainty that the story was not over.

"Why": As Jesus calls to God, he asks the same question everyone who has ever believed asks: "Why?" Our greatest temptation is to know the things of God. That was the first temptation offered to Adam and Eve. As mortal creatures, we are pressed with questions of immortality. Why does God act in some situations but remain silent in others? Why is he both so demanding and yet so loving? Why do the unjust succeed while the just suffer? Why did God create us knowing we would sin and suffer accordingly? Why sickness? Why pain? Why death? Why…?!

We are introduced to God in certain terms. We convert to the faith with the sure knowledge of our salvation. Those who admit they are sinners can believe in Jesus for salvation and confess their faith in him. Early in the faith, we learn of God's providence and

Step Four - Wrestling with God

plan for the world. His love is unending and his mercy without bounds. Each claim is true and held dear by the believer.

These are things we know about God. But to know God as a real actor in history is far more confusing. Throughout Scripture, we read that God does things that seem completely irrational.

> Why does God allow Satan in the garden?
> Why does God tell Abraham to kill Issac?
> Why isn't Moses allowed to enter the promised land after leading the Hebrew people for generations?
> Why have the people of Israel been carried into exile for generations?

With Job, we question the will of God when disaster comes. We wait to hear God in a whirlwind that usually never comes. When Jesus looked to heaven and asked "why," he joined the chorus of humanity that cries out to God for help and does not hear an immediate reply.

On Calvary, Jesus represented the hopeless, vulnerable peoples throughout history who have lacked freedom and power to act in their own best interests. The bulk of the world has been oppressed and alienated. Jesus cried out with them and for them, "My God, my God, why have you forsaken me?!"

Questioning God is not necessarily a sign of disbelief. Doubting the activity of God does not mean you are abandoning your faith. Rather, seeking to know the heart and mind of God will necessarily require questions. His ways are not our ways. We cannot fathom the mind of God. He is beyond our finite wisdom. Should we dare to inquire, we will undoubtedly be baffled and confused. The cross is the pinnacle of confusion. The most innocent man who ever lived was prosecuted and executed by a corrupted society. Not only did God allow this to happen, but it was all part of his plan. If we step back and look at the proceedings, we cannot help but ask, with Jesus, "Why?"

This word should give great comfort to all those who have questioned God. Perhaps you have prayed for a desired result, one that seemed obvious. Of course God would want to restore your marriage or heal your loved one, right? The answers do not come. God is silent.

It is at the cross that we can have both our greatest disillusionment and our greatest comfort. Because, while God is terribly silent, we know he is faithful. Some of the answers we seek on Good Friday cannot (and will not) be revealed until Easter Sunday. The blood and despair of the cross seemed pointless and confusing. But the mastery of God's plan came into full view in light of the empty tomb. With Jesus, we can look to heaven and ask why with the full assurance that God is faithful, and his plan and providence are truly good.

"Have you forsaken me?": In this moment of darkness, Jesus was forsaken by God. It is hard to grasp the gulf that was created on Calvary to implore Jesus to ask, "Why have you forsaken me?"

One of my earliest childhood memories is in the airport in Newark, New Jersey. It was the Thanksgiving holiday in one of the busiest airports in the country. I was four years old, the youngest of my three siblings. We were rushing through the shoulder-to-shoulder holiday travelers, trying to get to a connecting flight to visit family in Massachusetts. In the bustle, I glanced at a gift shop and saw toy airplanes dangling in the window. I let go of my dad's hand to have a look. When I turned around, my family was gone. I was lost.

The next several minutes are a blur. I remember a very nice airport employee asking me if I was lost. (The tears were a clue.) He sat me on an airport cart and took me to the center station to make the "did someone lose a child" announcement. While we waited, he let me stand on the baggage mover.

The next thing I remember, my mom charged toward me, with tears in it's eyes, and picked me up in her arms. She was trembling, but (to my relief), she wasn't mad. We were reunited. Everything was fine. The whole ordeal lasted maybe five minutes. Those were five excruciating minutes for my parents. Decades later, my parents and I vividly remember these moments of separation, even though it was a relatively short time. Even a few moments of separation between parent and child seem endless.

Jesus was forsaken, alone, and separated from his Father. It is impossible to articulate the depth of sorrow swelling in his heart. The fourth cry from the cross was more than an emotional plea from Son to Father. This was not simply a "feeling" that Jesus was enduring.

Theologically speaking, God had forsaken Jesus on the cross. But why? Why must God forsake his Son?

On Calvary, Jesus bore the sin of the world. He became our sin. Before the cross, Jesus was in perfect unison and harmony with the Father. He had never sinned and lived in perfect obedience. Jesus went to the cross to bear our sins. In doing so, he incurred the punishment that we deserved. We are the ones who have sinned and offended God, but Jesus took the punishment.

There is an old story from the Middle Ages about the king of the Francs. When he first heard the story of Jesus, he was taken aback: "If my army were there, we would never let that man be crucified!" But the king was wrong. His sin, and our sin, put Jesus on the cross. Our sin requires punishment, lest we face the wrath of God. The holiness of God is such that no person can bear it in a sinful condition. A sacrifice must be made before we can enter the presence of God.

In the Old Testament, God revealed the means by which people could receive his forgiveness. A blood sacrifice was required in order to atone for the sins of the people. Blood from unblemished animals was spilled to make recompense for the offenses against God. These bloody rituals were to be repeated year after year.

When Jesus began his ministry, John the Baptist called out, "Behold, the Lamb of God who takes away the sins of the world!"[26] Jesus was announced as the perfect, unblemished sacrifice that would take on our sins and bear them on Calvary's cross. But redemption could not be accomplished without the shedding of blood. The Messiah would be a sacrificial lamb. Jesus became the curse of sin and the sacrifice for our redemption.

Paul told the Galatian church:

Christ redeemed us from the curse of the law by becoming a curse for us...[27]

Jesus became the curse, and in doing so, he bore the punishment that we deserved. When Jesus became sinful, God the Father could not remain in harmony and unison with him as before. God had to turn away from his Son, to forsake him, because he was carrying sin. The only person God has ever forsaken was his Son. It was a terrible moment of literal and spiritual darkness. But because he was forsaken, we are redeemed.

Paul wrote of this triumph to the Corinthian church:

> *God made him who had no sin to be sin for us, so that in him we might become the righteousness of God.*[28]

We must be careful here. The work of atonement on the cross has led some to consider God a wrathful, bloodthirsty tyrant who demanded the blood of his Son in order to be satisfied. But this image is not accurate. Because God loves the world, he sent the only one who could offer perfect redemption to the world. The cross is a marker of just how much God desires to be reconciled with us. We are so valuable to him, and his love is so great, that he sent his very heart, his only begotten Son.[29]

Jesus reciprocated this love to the Father. He was aware of the necessity of the cross and willing to endure this suffering. He was not coerced or persuaded into Calvary. Because of his great love, Jesus submitted himself to crucifixion for our redemption. Both God the Father and Jesus acted out of love and mutual submission to one another. And all this was for our benefit.

As John Stott wrote:

> *We must not, then, speak of God punishing Jesus or of Jesus persuading God, for to do so is to set them over against each other as if they acted independently of each other or were even in conflict with each other.... The Father did not lay on the Son an ordeal he was reluctant to bear, nor did the Son extract from the Father a salvation he was reluctant to bestow.*[30]

When we hear the fourth cry from the cross, and listen to Jesus's desperation that comes with distance from God, we know it is for our redemption. Jesus bore our curse on Calvary:

> *'He himself bore our sins' in his body on the cross, so that we might die to sins and live*
>
> *for righteousness; 'by his wounds you have been healed.'*[31]

Further, Jesus was forsaken in order to relate to those who are forsaken in a broken world, those who have felt abandoned by God. His cry, as desperate as it was, was not hopeless. He knew resurrection was coming.

As we journey closer to the heart of God, we can be reminded that it is essential to grapple with God. While we tend to solve our problems with words and actions, God often remains silent. As we mature in our faith, we can learn to live in the silence and trust his plans, even when we do not see him moving. He will act, most often in ways we do not expect. Someone once said, God always says yes to our prayers or he has something better. He may not answer in the way we expect, but he will answer.

At *Step Four: Wrestling with God*, we are reminded of the unending faithfulness of God and how we need to hold onto hope, even when we are feeling forsaken. Sometimes we need to cry out into the silence with frustrated tones and beg him to answer. He may not speak while we suffer. God is often mysterious and silent. But the empty tomb is a reminder that God always keeps his promises in his time.

---

[1] Mark 15:34; Matthew 27:46
[2] Luke 22:54
[3] Matthew 27:45
[4] John 1:5
[5] Luke 23:44-45
[6] Exodus 10:21-29
[7] John 8:12
[8] Matthew 5:14-16
[9] Luke 15:8-10
[10] Matthew 6:19
[11] Matthew 25:31–46
[12] Matthew 25:1-13
[13] Matthew 8:12, 22:13, 25:30
[14] Isaiah 9:2, Matthew 4:16

[15] George Fox, *The Journal of George Fox*. (Richmond, IN: Friends United Press, 1997). 57.

[16] Matthew 27:51

[17] Matthew 27:46

[18] Matthew 7:9-11

[19] Matthew 6:25-27

[20] James Strong, *Strong's Expanded Exhaustive Concordance of the Bible* (Nashville: Thomas Nelson, 2009), s.v. "aneboēsen"

[21] John 20:29

[22] https://oldarchive.godspy.com/reviews/Finding-Joy-in- the-Darkest-Night-The-Divine-Abandonment-of-Mother-Teresa-by-David-Scott.cfm.htm

[23] Psalm 22:1-2

[24] Warren W. Wiersbe, *The Cross of Jesus: What His Words from Calvary Mean for Us*. (Grand Rapids, MI: Baker Publishing, 1997). Kindle Edition. Loc 1053.

[25] Psalm 22:22-24

[26] John 1:36

[27] Galatians 3:13

[28] 2 Corinthians 5:21

[29] John 3:16

[30] Erwin W. Lutzer, *Cries from the Cross: A Journey into the Heart of Jesus* (Chicago: Moody Publishers, 2015), Kindle Edition. 73.

[31] 1 Peter 2:24

Step Five - New Thirst

"I am thirsty."
John 19:28

While doing mission work in rural Jamaica, I got a glimpse into the necessity of clean water. In modern American society, all our basic physical necessities are met. We forget our primitive need for water. We are fortunate to have clean drinking water at the turn of a faucet. This privilege was not available for most of human history. Clean water is a necessity still not afforded to more than 800 million people in the world. For many in the developing world, the only water sources are shared with animals and used as latrines.

On the way home from one of our work projects, we stopped at a spring in the jungle, off the beaten path. As we approached the water source, a large Jamaican man came and peered in our direction. Most Jamaicans are very friendly and hospitable. In another circumstance, I am sure this fella was jovial. But he glared at us. As we approached the spring, he came over and told us, in no uncertain terms, which side of the spring we could use. One side was for cleaning, the other for drinking. We all got the message, loud and clear. This small spring was a life source for the community. If we carelessly put our dirty hands or feet in the wrong side, we would contaminate their water. The Jamaican was tasked with keeping the clumsy missionaries in line. When it came to their water, there were no more niceties. I cannot blame them. That small spring was their life.

Most of us have never experienced a severe thirst. The closest I have come to genuine, heart-wrenching thirst was during a summer half-marathon. In the middle of the race, a large gust of wind blew over a table full of water cups. That meant I had to run about five miles in the heat without a sip of water. I remember the desire for water encompassed my whole body in a way that I had never experienced. As my body became overwhelmed with thirst, I became furious. I could not think of anything else but my thirst.

I am told the Swedish word for thirst also means fire.[1] I believe it. I could not think about anything else. When I stumbled in to the water stop and had my first drink, all of my harsh emotions subsided. I did not care about the race anymore. I just wanted to drink. After just a short time without water, thirst consumes the mind and tears at the body. We are fortunate because we rarely experience severe dehydration.

In *Step Four: Wrestling with God*, we learn to trust God, even when we grapple with him. Here we come to *Step Five: New Thirst*. At this stage, we begin to long, or thirst, for the things of God. As we grow deeper in our relationship with God, we begin to mirror his heart. We want the things of God. We want love and reconciliation. We want justice for the vulnerable. Our hearts are broken by the things that break the heart of God.

Too many believers never reach this stage in their spiritual development. Their longings never change. They commit the same sins, and their desires remain the same. But those who take the next step in their spiritual lives are in for an adventure. They begin to thirst for the things of God. Jesus said to his disciples: "Blessed are those who hunger and thirst for righteousness."[2]

Those with a new thirst are satisfied in Christ, but never complacent. The "thirsty" Christians are those who are always pushing the church to see the real needs of their community and to become the hands and feet of Jesus.

The Shortest Word

"I am thirsty": The fifth word from the cross is also the shortest. The Greek rendering is actually one word, dipsaó (διψάω). Like many Greek verbs, dipsaó has a double meaning. The most common use of the word is physical. To dipsaó is to want something to drink. However, the word can also mean "desire earnestly."[3] As we will see, when Jesus said, "I am thirsty," it was both a physical and spiritual longing.

All of heaven and earth is addressed from the cross. Up to this point, Jesus had spoken to several people from the cross. His audience had included criminals, saints, family, and God. In the remaining words from the cross, Jesus will speak primarily about himself. The fifth word ("I am thirsty") is about his physical and spiritual longings, while the sixth ("It is finished") and seventh ("Into your hands") words are about his desire to finish the work God has for him.

Prophecy Fulfilled

When Jesus said from the cross that he was thirsty, it was the fulfillment of yet another prophecy. John records the scene:

> *Later, knowing that everything had now been finished, and so that Scripture would be fulfilled, Jesus said, 'I am thirsty.' A jar of wine vinegar was there, so they soaked a sponge in it, put the sponge on a stalk of the hyssop plant, and lifted it to Jesus' lips.*[4]

To ask for something to drink is very human. But like the entire life and ministry of Jesus, there was a deeper meaning. This word from Jesus was the fulfillment of a prophecy foretold hundreds of years before Calvary. Centuries earlier, the psalmist said of the Messiah:

> *They put gall in my food and gave me vinegar for my thirst.*[5]

The soldiers overseeing the crucifixion likely supplied the wine vinegar to Jesus. For them, giving him the sponge was a mundane act. Wine vinegar was cheap, common fare among the soldiers. They drank the concoction throughout the day as they tended to the condemned. They had to be there all day to oversee the gruesome demise of the crucified, and they brought food and drink to carry them through the day. This simple act, so trivial to the soldiers, was actually part of the divine fabric weaved over history. Here we see the interaction of God and history. We cannot comprehend the complexity and beauty of God's careful orchestration.

Everyone in the Scriptures was acting in their own self-interest. They were going about their business, seeking to do what they thought was right. All the while, God was using their actions to bring salvation for the entire world.

In betraying Jesus, could Judas have known he was a key player in Jesus's crucifixion and therefore the salvation of the world? Could the religious leaders have comprehended that their long hatred of Jesus would lead to his arrest and eventually the saving work of the cross? Could Pilate have known that the sentencing of Jesus, carried out by his Roman executioners, was making a way for salvation for the whole world?

Of course not.

There is much debate about why they gave Jesus the wine vinegar. Were they compassionate? Were they mocking him? Did they want to hear what else he would say? They are all viable theories. Whatever their motives, God's plan was greater. The passion narrative played out in a way that completed God's plan for the redemption of the world. God fulfills his promises, and humanity is a bit player in the action.

The next time you think your life in Christ may not matter, remember the soldiers giving Jesus wine vinegar. Something rote and routine was fulfilling a providential purpose. You may think your time in prayer, service, teaching Sunday school, preaching the sermons, or doing whatever your role is in the kingdom is not having an impact. But God could be using your life to impact someone else for all of eternity!

Another detail is often overlooked in this passage. Before the wine vinegar was lifted to Jesus's lips, it was put on a sponge on a stalk of "hyssop plant."[6] This is a significant detail that would have resonated with faithful Jews.

Hundreds of years before, when the Hebrew people were in captivity in Egypt, God sent an angel of death over the entire land. Only those who spread blood of a sacrificed animal over their door frames were spared. The Hebrews were instructed to use hyssop plants to paint blood on their doors.[7] The angel of death "passed over" the doors with sacrificial blood.

When we fast forward to the cross, we see the divine juxtaposition. He who would cleanse the world of their sins was offered hyssop. Earlier in the gospel of John, Jesus said, "I am the gate," that is, the doorway of entry.[8] On the cross, the gateway to God—Jesus Christ—is brushed with hyssop.

His Humanity

The fifth word from the cross put the humanity of Jesus on full display. Hours of trial and suffering made Jesus physically thirsty. The night before, he had labored in prayer in Gethsemane. Luke tells us that the anxiety about the coming physical suffering was so great that Jesus sweat blood.[9] That same night, he was betrayed by his disciples and set before an unjust court.[10] The next day Jesus was put before the Romans and sentenced by a mob to crucifixion.[11] He was betrayed, harangued, and tired. His body labored and his emotions drained, Jesus was thirsty.

Things only got more difficult. He was flogged with a cat-o-nine tails, a leather whip outfitted with shards of bone to tear the flesh. He received at least thirty-nine lashings from his shoulders to his buttocks. They placed a crown of thorns on him to mock him, which created a steady stream of blood down into his eyes and mouth. By this point, Jesus was bleeding from everywhere.

To dull the pain, Jesus was offered a sedative, but he refused.[12] From the cross, Jesus was experiencing the full brunt of pain. He endured every punch, lash, and stab so he could relate to our suffering. As the author of Hebrews would go on to say:

> *During the days of Jesus' life on earth, he offered up prayers and petitions with fervent cries and tears to the one who could save him from death, and he was heard because of his reverent submission.*[13]

The frailty of Jesus is hard for people to grasp, especially when he seems to have whimpered for water. The philosopher Friedrich Nietzsche, who famously claimed, "God is dead," mocked the idea of God on a cross and compared him to a limp spider in a web.[14]

One of the earliest Christian heresies was docetism, which claimed that Jesus only "appeared" (δοκεῖν/dokeĩn) to be human. Its followers believed Jesus was only a spiritual being because God would never allow himself to be subject to the actual indignities of the cross. It is hard to blame the docetists. Does anyone really want to worship a Savior who is parched and frail?

Even well-meaning Christians tend to over-spiritualize Jesus. Sure, he was human, but not like we are, right? Many believe that Jesus may have shared our experience, but he was not human in the fullest sense of the word. But the words "I am thirsty" lay waste to the notion of a super-human Jesus.

The One who was present at creation, hovering over the waters, was now longing for water. Jesus is the Master of the Storm, who can calm the sea and the weather, and now he was parched. The One who walked on water longed for a drink. When hungry, Jesus did not turn stones to bread. Jesus remained hungry in order to endure temptation for us and with us. Now, though he could have created a geyser of cold water, he remained thirsty to share in our experience.

From the cross, Jesus reached into our human condition and experienced our longings. In writing to the Philippian church, Paul would write of the kenosis (ἐκένωσεν/ekénōsen), or self-emptying, of Jesus. From the cross, Jesus:

> *made himself nothing by taking the very nature of a servant, being made in human likeness.*[15]

The second person in the Trinity, co-equal in glory with God, descended and became human. This was not a mirage or a semblance of humanity. He bore the entire weight of our condition, even enduring the worst of what we offer:

> *And being found in appearance as a man, he humbled himself by becoming obedient to death—even death on a cross!*[16]

How close is God? He is with us on Calvary. We may not feel the immediate presence of God in our life at all times. But he is there. He knows the hurt we feel in betrayal. He knows hunger. He knows what it is to suffer a grave injustice. Jesus got tired, angry, irritated, and even had multiple conflicts with his immediate family! Jesus knows our condition. On the cross, he became thirsty with us.

Thirst and Longing

That Jesus joined our humanity is a miracle to ponder. But the very fact that we thirst is, in itself, a sign of our broken world. We thirst because we have unmet desires. We are unfulfilled because sin is in the world. When God created Adam and Eve in the garden, everything was "good." In God's garden, there was peace, harmony, order, and satisfaction. There was never a mention of thirst. When humanity fell into sin, an imbalance was created that caused a longing that could not be satisfied. The human spirit is always longing for something else, something more. God created us to be satisfied in him, but sin has broken that key relationship. Now we always long for more.

A popular advertisement says, "Stay thirsty, my friends," as if we have another option. Everyone is thirsty for something. The question is not whether we thirst; rather, how are we going to satisfy our thirst?

Those around the cross had thirsts they were trying to satisfy: Judas was thirsty for money, so he sold information about Jesus's location for thirty pieces of silver. Herod was thirsty for power, so he oversaw the oppression and injustice of the Roman occupation. The disciples were thirsty for safety, so they fled the moment things became dangerous.

Jesus often taught about people who had unmet longings: In the parable of the prodigal son, the younger brother was thirsty for a wild, carefree life. He returned home to find the satisfaction for which he truly longed. The rich, young ruler was longing for a deeper walk with God, but refused to give up his material possessions. He did not want the waters that satisfy. Nicodemus was thirsty for the teachings of Jesus, but was ashamed to be seen with him. So he ventured to meet with him at night. In each instance, Jesus offered a life with God as the only way of satisfaction. Of course, the thing we need most is often the one most neglected.

Jesus's encounter with the Samaritan woman is a vivid account of someone who had a longing in her life.[17] Jesus and his disciples were traveling through Samaria, which was a scandalous journey on its own. Jews and Samaritans did not typically associate with one another. While the disciples had gone into town to buy something to eat, Jesus went to a well to get a drink.

While there, he encountered a Samaritan woman who was drawing water. Jesus asked her, "Will you give me something to drink?"[18] This question was audacious, as Jesus was alone and speaking with a woman. Evidence suggests the woman probably thought Jesus was being rude, even in asking. The conversation continued:

> *You are a Jew and I am a Samaritan woman. How can you ask me for a drink?*[19]

Jesus said,

> *If you knew the gift of God and who it is that asks you for a drink, you would have asked him and he would have given you living water.*[20]

The Samaritan woman did not understand what Jesus was saying. In an earlier scene, Jesus took a few loaves of bread and turned it into enough to feed the multitude. This was a sign that Jesus is the new manna, the bread of heaven. But the multitude was not concerned with the spiritual significance. They wanted Jesus to supply their physical needs. They wanted an endless supply of bread and fish. The Samaritan woman was drawing a similar conclusion. She wanted actual H_2O. She replied, hopeful of an unending spring to draw water:

> *Sir…you have nothing to draw with and the well is deep. Where can you get this living water?*[21]

In Jesus's reply, he told her of water that would satisfy the spirit:

> *Everyone who drinks this water will be thirsty again, but whoever drinks the water I give them will never thirst. Indeed, the water I give them will become in them a spring of water welling up to eternal life.*[22]

Hearing this good news, the Samaritan replied:

> *Sir, give me this water so that I won't get thirsty and have to keep coming here to draw water.*[23]

It is here that Jesus changed the conversation. He spoke to her spiritual longings. The Samaritan woman was only referencing her physical, superficial thirst. But Jesus pried deeper:

> *Go, call your husband and come back.*[24]

Jesus peered into her heart. He knew she had had five husbands and was now in a relationship with a man to whom she was not married.[25] This was not to embarrass or shame the Samaritan woman. The fact that she had to come alone to the well in the middle of the day is evidence that the community had already abandoned her. Rather, Jesus knew that this woman had been trying to quench her spiritual thirst in all the wrong wells. Her relationships were not meeting her inward need. Jesus named this longing and offered her living water from a well that never runs dry.

When we come to Jesus, we encounter a Savior who offers satisfying, living water. The old wells won't do anymore. We seek to satisfy our spiritual longings in a lot of different ways. Those who feel a deep desire to be liked will drink from the well of relationships. Those who long for safety and security drink from the well of success. The pleasure-seekers among us may drink from the well of addiction. Every one leaves us thirsty. Jesus calls us close to himself because, in him, we find the water that satisfies.

Psalm 42 speaks of the deep longing of the soul:

> *As the deer pants for streams of water, so my soul pants for you, my God. My soul thirsts for God, for the living God. When can I go and meet with God?*[26]

Step Five - New Thirst

This longing for God is at the heart of every person. It has been said we all have "a God-shaped hole." Sadly, most try to fill that emptiness with material or emotional goods. But to try to satisfy a spiritual longing with a material indulgence only leads to more thirst.

In Luke 16, Jesus gave a terrifying depiction of hell. A wealthy man had died and gone to hell, while his servant Lazarus went to heaven. The wealthy man cried out to Abraham and begged him to send his servant Lazarus to bring just a taste of water. In desperation he said:

> *Have pity on me and send Lazarus to*
> *dip the tip of his finger in water and*
> *cool my tongue because I am in*
> *agony in this fire!*[27]

Hell is described as a place of eternal thirst, eternal longing that cannot be satisfied. The story goes on to say that the wealthy man had enjoyed the finer things of life and never considered eternity. At death, the "great chasm" was set in place and could not be bridged. The wealthy man was condemned to thirst for all eternity.

We contrast this image of thirst in hell with satisfaction in heaven. The book of Revelation offers a vision of heaven with satisfying waters. In chapter 7, we read that all the faithful are gathered around the throne, completely satisfied in eternal worship of Christ:

> *Never again will they hunger;*
> *never again will they thirst.*
> *The sun will not beat down on them,*
> *nor any scorching heat.*
>
> *For the Lamb at the center of the*
> *throne will be their shepherd;*
> *he will lead them to springs of living*
> *water.*
>
> *And God will wipe away every tear*
> *from their eyes.*[28]

Heaven is eternal satisfaction. The unmet longings that served as a catalyst for so much of our earthly life will be gone. The faithful are satisfied in Christ with every thirst perfectly quenched. This is the great promise for those who partake of the Living Water!

The Cups Offered to Jesus

Warren Wiersbe highlights the cups that were offered to Jesus.[29] Each one represents the ways we try to make amends with God. The cup of gall offered is a sign of sympathy.[30] Some believe that if they are sympathetic to the cause of the needy, they are justified before God. Just having a sensation of empathy for the poor is enough. Others offer a cup of charity. Like the soldiers who offered Jesus myrrh as a sedative, many believe that they can buy their way into heaven. If you give enough of your time and money, the thought goes, you can earn your way into heaven. I wish I had a nickel for every time someone told me they were "basically a good person." They come to this conclusion based on their own calculation of generosity versus selfishness. In reality, all of the good deeds in the world do not cover our sinful offenses before God.

Thankfully, Jesus brought the perfect cup to God: the cup of iniquity. When the disciples foolishly declared that they would die with Jesus, he said to them, "Can you drink the cup I drink or be baptized with the baptism I am baptized with?"[31]

They could not drink that cup. No one can. Jesus was referencing his baptism of death and the victory of the resurrection. Jesus drank from the cup of iniquity and, because of his suffering and death, we are redeemed in the sight of God.

We should bring an empty cup to Jesus. In humility and brokenness, we come to Jesus as empty vessels. The hardest thing to do is to come before God empty handed. We want to offer something, anything to God. But in reality, the only offering we have is a pittance to a God who demands holiness.

Come, All Who are Thirsty

Step Five: New Thirst is an invitation for us to embrace the humanity of Jesus. In him, we encounter a Savior who has fully embraced our condition with all its hurt and pain. This is not a distant, aloof God. He is near to us in the person and work of Jesus Christ. Because he became as we are, and endured terrible pain, we can take confidence when trial and suffering come our way. Few people have suffered for the Christian faith like Paul. But Paul did not lament or complain about his suffering. Rather, he believed his pain was serving a greater purpose in glorifying Christ in him:

> *We always carry around in our body the death of Jesus, so that the life of Jesus may also be revealed in our body.*[32]

In a world that treats pain as a problem to be fixed, rather than a natural part of life, Christians should use our suffering to glorify God. As a pastor, I have sat at many hospital bedsides with people in terrible pain. Some have had sudden illnesses or accidents, and others deal with long-term conditions. Those who are mature in faith may have some worry and anxiety, but they know that God is faithful in both trial and suffering. He is God, whether it is Good Friday or Easter morning.

The church is a well from which spiritually thirsty people can drink. After all, we offer Living Water that always satisfies the spirit. Sadly, churches have a reputation for serving the same old drinks of the world: religiosity, bitterness, consumerism, division, etc... But I believe God has a greater purpose for his church: to offer the drink that satisfies for all eternity.

God Became Thirsty

My dad has never been healthy. He is a very good man and raised his family to the best of his abilities. Because of his severe bipolar disorder, Dad would need constant medication and counsel to maintain a semblance of a healthy life. And, bless him, he did the best he could. Though crowds were always difficult for Dad, he never missed any of our ballgames. He gave us pocket money while we were in college and broke. Given the circumstances, I couldn't have asked for more.

As the years wore on, Dad's health continued to deteriorate. A constant stream of medication had adverse effects. The doctors who tended to Dad were mostly ambivalent about his care. It is easy to see why. He did not say much and rarely complained. When he did talk, it was terse and awkward. Dad developed a tremor in his hands that was written off as a symptom of his medicines. It was later diagnosed as Parkinson's.

Dad developed hydrocephalus, which was caused by the accumulation of spinal fluid in his skull. The pressure meant he lost most of his basic abilities, including walking, dexterity, and feeding himself. At sixty-eight years old, when many are enjoying their golden years, Dad is confined to a wheelchair and hardly able to communicate. In a last-ditch attempt to recover some of his lost faculty, we took the doctor's recommendation to have a shunt put in his spinal cord. This would, in theory, create an opportunity for the fluid to flush and restore some of Dad's capacity.

As anyone who has undergone a surgery knows, patients are not allowed to eat or drink for twelve hours before. I went through the rigmarole of getting Dad to the hospital for an 8 a.m. surgery. He did not get called back until 2 p.m. The last hours were the worst. All he could say, over and again, was "thirsty." He repeated it over and again: "thirsty, thirsty, thirsty…" Every other desire had ceased.

My dad's body has failed him. His mind is gone. In his frail state, he can only express some very basic thoughts. On the day of his surgery, he said over and again: thirsty, thirsty, thirsty.

Part of my consolation with my dad is in knowing that Jesus is there in my dad's suffering. Jesus has been confined. He was dehydrated. Jesus was thirsty. The good news is that my dad knows Christ in his heart. He has enjoyed the cup of salvation. Though he may be feeble now, one day my dad will join the heavenly chorus and praise God from a place of complete satisfaction. Jesus became thirsty so that my father could enjoy the eternal drink.

At Calvary, God became like my dad. He became like every other person in the world who suffers without their most basic faculties. Jesus suffered with the whole of humanity who has cried out for physical, spiritual, and social satisfaction. The incarnation of Jesus (the term for God becoming man) sets Christianity apart from every other religion. Other religions have heroes who achieve a physical or moral heroism that is beyond our grasp. Rather than becoming a champion or warrior to save us from enemies, God entered our condition. He became as we are, enduring the frail vessel of our flesh. As such, Jesus took on all the indignities of our emotions. Though he never sinned, Jesus did become angry, tired, and as we see on the cross…thirsty. This simple phrase, "I am thirsty," is a sign of Emmanuel, God with us.[33]

As we journey to the heart of God, seeking a more mature walk with him, our desires should transform. At *Step Five: New Thirst*, the regenerative work of the Holy Spirit leads the believer to new desires. Instead of selfishness, we seek the best for others. We develop a heart for the poor and vulnerable, a restless thirst for justice. We invite others to the living water of Jesus, knowing that he has quenched our greatest desires. As Augustine said, "Our souls are restless until they rest in thee." The source of every longing is spiritual and no temporal drink will satisfy our inward desires. Jesus became thirsty on the cross so that we may have satisfaction in him. As we drink from the Living Water, we develop a new, insatiable thirst for the desires of God.

---

[1] Erwin W. Lutzer, *Cries from the Cross: A Journey into the Heart of Jesus* (Chicago: Moody Publishers, 2015), Kindle Edition. 88.

[2] Matthew 5:6

[3] James Strong, *Strong's Expanded Exhaustive Concordance of the Bible* (Nashville: Thomas Nelson, 2009), s.v. "dipsaó"

[4] John 19:28-29

[5] Psalm 69:21

[6] John 19:29

[7] Exodus 12:22

[8] John 10:9

[9] Luke 22:44

[10] Luke 22:66-23:25

[11] Matthew 27:22, Mark 15:13, Luke 23:21

[12] Matthew 27:34

[13] Hebrews 5:7

[14] John Stott. *The Cross of Christ*. (Downers Grove, IL: IVP Books, 2006). 47.

[15] Philippians 2:7

[16] Philippians 2:8

[17] John 4:1-26

[18] John 4:7
[19] John 4:9
[20] John 4:10
[21] John 4:11
[22] John 4:13-14
[23] John 4:15
[24] John 4:16
[25] John 4:18
[26] Psalm 42:1-2
[27] Luke 16:24
[28] Revelation 7:14-16
[29] Warren W. Wiersbe, *The Cross of Jesus: What His Words from Calvary Mean for Us*. (Grand Rapids, MI: Baker Publishing, 1997). Kindle Edition. Loc 1155.
[30] Matthew 27:34
[31] Mark 10:28
[32] 2 Corinthians 4:10
[33] Matthew 1:23

Step Six - Confidence in Salvation

"It is finished."
John 19:30

Emily and I decided we were just going to do the thing we always wanted to do. We were going to stop dreaming about it and start planning: We were going to build a house.

This had long been a dream of ours. As newlyweds, we imagined our "forever" house. We imagined the design and features we would enjoy in our home.

Then reality set in. We started a family, and the kids kept coming: four! Our dream of building a house never materialized. When our youngest was (finally) out of diapers, Emily and I started speaking to one another again. Parents of small children know what I'm talking about. When you have toddlers, you are in survival mode. The goal is to make it to bedtime. It does not leave much time for visioning about a mudroom.

My wife and I did not have an adult conversation for about a decade. I'm joking of course, but we did not talk about the idea of building a house for a long time. Once things calmed down, we dusted off our old dream. We set to work and, with a little luck, we were able to buy a plot of land in the area where we wanted to live.

Up to that point in my life, I had never considered how a house gets built. I assumed they fell from the sky. I was not expecting the endless barrage of decisions to make when designing and building a house. I am not complaining (well, not anymore). It is a tremendous privilege to build a house. But, boy, were there a lot of questions.

Where do we put the house on the lot? How many rooms? Materials? Wood? Vinyl? Carpet? Paint colors? Light fixtures? Mailbox? Concrete? Countertops? Light switches? Hardwood floors? Furniture? And on and on and on! Fortunately for me (and everyone who lives in the house), my wife has a knack for this kind of thing. She answered the brunt of the questions.

After months of anticipation, our house was finished. I will never forget the day we got approval from the county inspector. We could finally move in! It was done. Finished. Our dream had come true. We were done with the house!

Except, we weren't done. That feeling of completion was short lived. As soon as we moved in, we needed to unpack. As we unpacked, we needed to hang up pictures. After that, another round of sorting. As I write, we are moved in and getting settled, but we are still working on the house. We are in, but we are not finished.

Are we ever "finished"? Is anything ever done?

The most significant moments of life are usually gateways to a new chapter in life. Nothing is finished. When we finish our education, we begin a career, another phase of the journey. A wedding does not complete the relationship, but begins the marriage. Nothing, it seems, is ever truly finished. Only fairy tales and sit-coms end with a tidy "happily ever after." In real life, the journey presses on from one chapter to another, ending one phase only to begin another.

Yet in the midst of our seemingly endless transitions in life, Jesus stuns us with this sixth word from the cross:

It is finished.[1]

This word heralds the finished work of God in Jesus Christ. Our salvation is fixed. God completed the work. There is nothing we can do to add to this opus. The sixth word from the cross represents a place of spiritual security in our walk with Christ. As we mature in our walk with God, we come to a realization of God's finished work in Jesus Christ. That does not mean that we are finished! Quite the contrary. As long as we remain in sinful flesh, we are on a natural bent away from God. But the claim "it is finished" tells us there is nothing we can do to further our redemption. As we grow in Christ, we overcome the temptation to add to our salvation. Mature believers know that, because of the cross, salvation is complete.

We are tempted to try to add to the work of the cross. Sure, we are saved, but don't we have to fulfill certain religious requirements? We need to dress and speak a certain way. We need to be offended at the right things. Religious observation becomes the marker of spiritual depth. We are reminded that the Pharisees hated Jesus not because of his devotion to God, but because his disciples did not properly wash their hands.[2] They plucked grain on the wrong day.³ Jesus had supper with the wrong people.⁴ How can Jesus be holy if he is not practicing the correct rituals? The Pharisees could not understand. Neither can many Bible-believing Christians. Our salvation is not dependent upon our precise observance. The work of God is finished in Christ.

Jesus's words, "It is finished," represent *Step Six: Confidence in Salvation*. Christians who make this step in their spiritual lives have found security in Christ's finished work. These saints make every effort to live a holy and righteous life. They flee from sin. They hold one another accountable. But it is not religious score-keeping. It is the confident pursuit of a life that pleases God in the knowledge that God has already finished the most important work. At *Step Six*, believers are free to pursue Christ without judging others or feeling as though they need to pass rigid religious tests. After all, the greatest work of God is "finished."

Tetelestai

"It is finished": Like the fifth word from the cross ("I thirst"), the sixth word is only one Greek word: tetelestai (τετέλεσται).⁵ But these one-word phrases are exact opposites. Jesus spoke of his thirst as an expression of his physical pain and spiritual longing. It was more of a concession about his human frailty and limitations. But the next phrase, "It is finished," is a proclamation of victory.

"It is finished" is a loaded phrase with profound meaning. The Greek "tetelestai" is a derivative of telos, which means "end, finish, conclude." Telos is used twenty-eight times in the New Testament and typically refers to the conclusion of a moment or action. Telos can also refer to the conclusion of an act or state of being. It is often used to reference the apocalypse or the "end of the age."

The term Jesus used was not telos, but tetelestai, which is only used twice in the New Testament. The other usage is in the verse just previous, "Later, knowing that everything had been finished..."⁶ This means a definite work that has been finalized, finished, completed. Tetelestai points to the specific work that God started being finalized in the cross. The Latin rendering is even more clear: "consummation est." The work of God is finished, culminated, completed...even consummated on Calvary's cross!

The sixth word from the cross is no small matter. God does not often declare something "finished." In the Old Testament, the "finished work" marked a key moment in God's interaction with the world. At creation, God declared his work complete or finished. The first verses from Genesis tell us that the world was a boundless abyss with no structure or purpose. In creation, God created lights to govern the days and nights, and raised up dry land to give the much-needed boundaries for the waters. The world would teem with living creatures that would multiply and, in their beauty, resound the glory of God.[7] God's first finished product was an end to chaos. On the seventh day, it was finished and God rested.[8]

Sin creates chaos, both in the spiritual and physical realms. Sin is the cause of our enmity with God and others. Sin causes disorder. But in Christ, there is peace. He has tamed the sting of death and given us a narrow path to follow.[9] In the same way that God raised dry land to bind the chaotic waters, so Christ has offered us peace in the midst of sin.

Another declaration of a finished work is in Exodus 40. God gave to Moses a long, detailed set of instructions for the Tabernacle. The Hebrew people had been rescued from Egyptian captivity and needed the means to worship God in the wilderness. Through several chapters in Exodus, Moses was given the design for the Tabernacle and the elements of worship within. At the end of the instructions, Moses "finished" the work.[10] This completed space of worship meant that God would not be distant from his people. He would be close to them through their worship.

Jesus is the both the object and aim of our worship. We do not rely on the rituals of the old covenant. The Hebrew people were given ornate, detailed instructions concerning the space of worship. But when Christ was crucified, the curtain in the Temple that separated the holiest place from the outer courts was torn in two. The presence of God was no longer held within a temple, behind an ornate set of sacrifices and rituals. Everyone who calls on the name of Jesus is privileged to come into the presence of God. Because of Jesus's finished work on the cross, we can "approach God's throne of grace with confidence, so that we may receive mercy and find grace to help us in our time of need."[11]

Another finished work of God is found in Joshua 19. The Hebrew people had searched for the promised land for generations.

They had become a nomadic people without a place to lay a foundation. At long last, the people of God were granted entry into the promised land. It was Joshua who led the people to the place they would live for generations. As God's people finally settled in to their new home, the work was declared "finished." This final declaration of completion was a defeat of homelessness.

The church on earth is the model for eternity. In Christ, we find our new settlement. Our homeland is not in the soil of an earthly boundary, but in heaven. We have become citizens of a kingdom beyond this world:

> *But our citizenship is in heaven. And we eagerly await a Savior from there, the Lord Jesus Christ.*[12]

The church is the temporary settlement where we prepare for our eternal home. We gather for worship, enjoy divine fellowship, and emanate the light of God to the world. Among the congregation of the faithful, we remind each other that we have a permanent home beyond this mortal world. In Christ, our destiny is secure. Indeed, "it is finished!"

A Familiar Phrase

It is no accident that Jesus used this particular word "tetelestai." It was common parlance used by people from every walk of life. When we unpack the variety of meanings in this word, we can see how it points to Jesus and his finished work on Calvary. Warren Wiersbe cites the different ways tetelestai was understood in Jesus's day[13]:

Servants: When asked to do a task by their master, faithful servants would get to work. Once the job was complete, the servant would find the master and proclaim "tetelestai," the work is done. Jesus was a faithful servant of God. He was perfect in obedience to his Father and never strayed from his divine will. The greatest, and most difficult, work that Jesus came to do was on Calvary. Jesus was declaring to his Father that the task he was given had now been completed.

Priests: The priests who were responsible for inspecting animals for sacrifice would declare "tetelestai." Sickly or blemished animals were not suitable for sacrifice.[14] But when a healthy animal was presented at the Temple, the priest would deem it worthy. Jesus was the unblemished sacrifice. When John the Baptist saw Jesus, he said, "Behold, the lamb of God who takes away the sin of the world."[15] That proclamation by John the Baptist was a testimony to the role that Jesus would play in our salvation. Jesus was the final offering to God. Under the old covenant, people were expected to bring a multitude of animals to the Temple for sacrifice, year after year. In Christ, the perfect offering has been given. As the author of Hebrews said, "For by one sacrifice he has made perfect forever those who are being made holy."[16] In proclaiming tetelestai, Jesus proclaimed that he was the unblemished, unending sacrifice.

Artists: Upon the last brushstroke, an artist could proclaim "tetelestai," the work is complete. Only the artist knows when the work is finished. The cross represents the final piece in God's tapestry of salvation. God had been weaving together a redemptive narrative throughout history. He had revealed the Law as unifying precepts for his people. The prophets foretold a culminating redemptive act. The feasts of the Old Testament foreshadowed a greater celebration. Even the history of God's people, through exile and return, points to the death and resurrection of Jesus. At the cross, God connected the dots. Everything in the old points to the new. It is a divine masterpiece. Jesus's proclamation, "It is finished," was the acknowledgment that the final piece had been added to the puzzle. The long history of Israel and God's plan for salvation was finished!

Merchants: Finally, merchants often used the term "tetelestai" to mark the end of a transaction. Multiple receipts and statements have been uncovered from the ancient world, and often "tetelestai" was written at the bottom. When a bill had been paid in full, the merchant would write, "It is paid." Jesus is the payment for our sins. We owe an insurmountable debt to God. In our sinful condition, we are unworthy to stand in his presence. I once heard a pastor tell of an encounter with a non-Christian. The spiritual-but-not-religious person said, "I'm looking forward to standing before God." The pastor gently replied, "It would be like standing 100 yards away from the sun."

It is impossible to express the majesty of God's holiness. He is perfect in glory, resplendent beyond words. We are flawed, finite, and blemished because of sin. On Calvary, Jesus offered the perfect payment for our sins. He is fully human, just like us. Jesus knows all our mortal flaws and suffered our temptations. And yet he is fully divine. Jesus is one with the Father in perfect unison and can therefore relate to his divinity. This makes him a perfect mediator for our sinful condition. In his blood, there is perfect redemption:

> *In him we have redemption through his blood, the forgiveness of sins, in accordance with the riches of God's grace.*[17]

The debt has been eliminated and paid in full by Jesus. It is finished!

What is "It"?

Jesus boldly proclaimed, "It is finished," which begs the question: What exactly is "it"? What was Jesus actually finishing on the cross? Some have speculated that Jesus was simply exhausted and saying, "OK, I'm done. That's all I have to offer." But that interpretation rings hollow. Jesus was finishing the work of God on multiple levels. Steven Furtick considers what "it" was[18]:

The suffering of the cross. Calvary was a long shadow over the life of Jesus. At his birth, Jesus was given the gift of myrrh by one of the wise men from the East. Myrrh is made of a thorny plant and is often used to lather a corpse. Talk about an awkward baby gift! When he was presented in the Temple, Mary was told that this child would "pierce her heart,"[19] a foreshadowing of Mary's pain at the foot of the cross. During his ministry, Jesus told his disciples that the Temple would be torn down and rebuilt in three days. This self-referential prophecy was an allusion to his painful death and victorious resurrection. In Gethsemane, Jesus considered whether the "cup" of judgment could be taken away.[20] He knew his life was heading to a painful death. After almost six long hours, Jesus could rightly proclaim, "It is finished." His suffering was over.

His life's work. Jesus was born with a unique task: to proclaim the Kingdom of God. This calling culminated with Calvary. Jesus went throughout the Judean countryside proclaiming the Kingdom of God. He preached good news to the poor. He performed miracles and exorcisms. People tried to make this into a public spectacle, as if Jesus were a sideshow performer. But Jesus always rejected showmanship. He even told people to keep his ministry a secret.[21] Jesus was a living, breathing image of God the Father. His mission was to embody the activity of God in the world. Jesus told his followers, "My food is to do the work of him who sent me."[22] Later he said, "For I have come down from heaven not to do my will but to do the will of him who sent me."[23] On Calvary, Jesus's work on earth was done. His ministry was done. His life's work was finished.

Fulfillment of Old Testament types. In theological parlance, a "type" is a theme, story, symbol, or image in the Old Testament that foreshadows Jesus in the New Testament. The Old Testament is always pointing toward the New. Jesus of Nazareth is the culmination of everything God was doing in the Old Testament. In his letter to the Romans, Paul acknowledged Jesus as a "type":

> *Death reigned from the time of Adam to the time of Moses, even over those who did not sin by breaking a command, as did Adam, who is a pattern (type/τύπος) of the one to come.*[24]

In the Garden of Eden, it was said that the serpent would be crushed by the offspring of Eve, but his heel would be bruised in the conflict.[25] This points to Christ, who defeated Satan but only by enduring the brutality of the cross.

When God condemned the world to a flood, he commanded Noah to build an ark that would save the righteous. Jesus is the ark of our salvation, and just as the boat was lifted off the ground by water, so we are lifted out of the water through baptism. God commanded Abraham to sacrifice his son. Scripture tells us that Isaac carried wood on his shoulders before he was to be slain. In the final moments, God rescinded the order and showed Abraham a ram that was caught in thorns.[26] This scene points to Christ who was not spared, but offered himself as a perfect sacrifice.

There are countless images in the Old Testament that point to Jesus. These types come into full color when viewed through the lens of the New Testament. What is whispered in the Old Testament becomes a victorious cry in the New: *It is finished!*

Fulfillment of the Law. The Law was offered by God to his people as a way of making them a unique people who were set apart from other nations. The Law was prized by the Hebrew people as "perfect, reviving the soul."[27] Those who meditate on the Law are: "like a tree planted by streams of water, which yields its fruit in season."[28] In their obedience to the Law, the Hebrew people would showcase the love and mercy of God to the entire world.

In the Law, God showed his concern for every aspect of life. Among other things, there was guidance on diet, cleanliness, sexual relations, rest and, of course, religious observance. God's people were to be unique in every facet of life. God's Law was the perimeters by which people could enjoy a good, fruitful, and peaceful life. Within the Law, the people of God were to have a special concern for the vulnerable. The poor, orphaned, widowed, and foreigners were to be included in the community of the faithful. But like all good things, the Law would be corrupted over time. People began to follow the Law out of obligation, rather than obedience. It became a weapon the religious elite would wield against the irreligious. And, most troubling, the poor were ignored or discarded by the people of Israel. God often reserved his most harsh judgment for Israel for when they neglected the vulnerable.

Jesus is the fulfillment of the Law. Jesus interpreted the Law in a way that was offensive to the religious leaders of the day. He insisted on obeying the "spirit" of the law. Following the letter of the Law does not equal devotion to God. Indeed, putting on a show of religiosity was abhorrent to God. The greatest, most consistent enemies of Jesus were the Pharisees. They were strict in their obedience to the Law and shunned those who did not follow it with their precision. Yet they neglected the premise of the Law. They worshiped the Law instead of adoring the Lawgiver. They performed their ceremonies to perfection, but neglected the most vulnerable.

Jesus said to his detractors, "I have not come to abolish the Law, but to fulfill the Law."[29] Jesus's interpretation of Scripture was not radical. It was simply a return to the original intention of the Law. Jesus never chastised anyone for doing their religious duty. Jesus kept kosher, fasted, and observed the Sabbath. But he did not do these religious exercises at the expense of the poor. Nor did he neglect the God of the Law. Jesus revealed what it looks like to follow the Law in a way that is pleasing to God. Jesus said "it is finished" to those who were obedient to the Law for their own selfish purposes. The Son of God came and followed the Law to its perfection. He is the fulfillment of the Law and the One who lived in perfect obedience to God.

The Truth about Jesus

At the cross, Jesus made claims that demand a response. There is no room for ambivalence. If Jesus is who he says he is, then we must make a choice. C.S. Lewis put it succinctly:

> *Either this man was, and is, the Son of God, or else a madman or something worse. You can shut him up for a fool, you can spit at him and kill him as a demon or you can fall at his feet and call him Lord and God, but let us not come with any patronizing nonsense about his being a great human teacher. He has not left that open to us. He did not intend to.*[30]

Some imagine Jesus as a soft moralizer who taught peace and harmony. This version of Jesus is acceptable to the masses. But Jesus is more than a good teacher. He made claims about himself as a "ransom for many," and he called himself the "Son of Man." The finished work of the cross bids us to see Jesus in full view. Here we must accept or reject the claims of Jesus:

Jesus is the Savior for the world. It is increasingly popular to refer to Jesus as a good teacher or strong moral example. Modern sentiment imagines that Jesus stands shoulder-to-shoulder with every other religious figure. But the cross tells a different story.

The proclamation "It is finished" tells the world that salvation does not come by any other name. Jesus is the only way to the Father. An acquaintance of mine once said to me, "I wish we could just scratch John 14:6." (That's where Jesus said, "I am the way and the truth and the life. No one comes to the Father except through me.") The gospel does not work that way. It is not ours to pick and choose. At the cross, we hear Jesus loudly and victoriously proclaim, "It is finished." The work of God is not accomplished by any other means. Salvation is through him alone.

We cannot add to our salvation. The sixth word tells us another important truth: the work of God is finished in Jesus Christ. We have a terrible tendency to add to the gospel message. Sure, salvation comes by faith, but you also have to do A, B, and C. The additions are different for every congregation. In my tradition, Quakers went through a generation where you were cast out if you did not marry within Friends congregations. Later, some were written off for failing to wear gray.

The opposition to Jesus's ministry did not come from the "heathens." The prostitutes, lepers, and tax collectors felt at ease with Jesus. He never condoned their sin, but he did not dispel them either. The Pharisees had animosity toward Jesus because he did not adhere to their strict religiosity.

The Pharisees committed a common sin. It is tempting to believe we must add to the work of God. But, as Jesus said, "It is finished." All of our good deeds and charity, when done to add assurance to our salvation, are fruitless. Charles Spurgeon said it well: "Why will you add your counterfeit farthing to the costly ransom which Christ has paid into the treasure-house of God?"[31]

God interacts with his creation. God is deeply involved in the workings of his creation. The Bible is a collection of stories that reveal a God who is highly involved in the world. He directs events toward his purposes. Some of these purposes are soon revealed, while it is generations before other events make sense. From the Garden of Eden to the cross and into eternity, God is engaged in the course of history.

Popular spirituality says that God is only semi-involved in the work of his creation. Sure, there is a god out there somewhere, but that god is not terribly concerned with our lives. As long as we maintain a semblance of "goodness" (whatever that means) and live a happy life, we are OK. In our world, it is perfectly appropriate to be "spiritual but not religious." That sentiment implies we can be our own god, forming our own morality as we shape our destiny.

But the God of the Bible and the Savior on the cross refute the spirit of the age. God is not a distant deity who is indifferent to the ways of the world. Rather, God has put a plan in motion, and he cares deeply about obedience and mercy. How we would love a disengaged god! If that were the case, we could do as we please.

On the cross, Jesus was proclaiming an end to God's work. The long history of revelation has reached a culmination on Calvary. This is not an "I'm OK, you're OK" spirituality. This is a rejection of fluid, boundless, chaotic, self-made mysticism. God revealed himself to the world through his people, the Law, prophets, and finally through his most perfect revelation: Jesus Christ. In him, the work of God was finished.

Is it Finished?

Just a little bit of wordplay turns Jesus's great proclamation into the great question of all humanity: "Is it finished?" There is, within all humanity, a lingering sense of restlessness. No matter how much we have, we always seem to want more. The work is never done. After the fall into sin in the Garden of Eden, Adam's labor became difficult. He was forced to break the hard ground and deal with the thorns. Work became burdensome instead of the delight that God intended. The laborious work is difficult and never done.

The most troubling question we all face is, "Is it finished?" That is, have I done what I am on earth to do? Have I lived according to my purpose? We apply this to our relationship with God as well. Am I good enough? Are my sympathy and charity and good deeds enough to please God? When I come to my end, is my work finished? In our long restlessness, we labor with the question, "Is it finished?!"

In the Garden of Eden, it was the devil who tempted Adam and Eve and fooled them into thinking that God had not done enough for them. God told them not to eat of the Tree of Knowledge. Satan told Adam and Eve that God made this requirement because, if they were to eat the fruit of this tree, they would know what God knows and become a threat to him. The first couple assumed God had not done enough. They asked, in effect, "Is it finished? Has God done everything he is going to do? Have I done enough?" They succumbed to the temptation and ate the forbidden fruit. Their sin was not just disobedience; it was being tricked into believing that they needed to do more to enjoy satisfaction with God.

Jesus answers the question in certain terms: tetelestai... "It is finished." Our salvation is fixed. As Paul said,

> *I have been crucified with Christ and I no longer live, but Christ lives in me. The life I now live in the body, I live by faith in the Son of God, who loved me and gave himself for me.*[32]

The work of God is done. There is nothing we can do to add to that which God has completed. As disciples grow in Christ, there needs to come a point of faithfulness where we too can declare with Jesus: It is finished. *Step Six: Confidence in Salvation* reminds us that there is nothing else we can do to add to our salvation. We continue to serve God and produce good fruit. We are persistent in proclaiming the gospel and sharing the light. But we do so knowing that this is the fruit of the spirit. By living the gospel life, we are not earning our salvation, we are expressing the grace of Christ within us.

---

[1] John 19:30

[2] Matthew 15:2, Luke 11:38

[3] Mark 2:23

[4] Matthew 11:19

[5] James Strong, *Strong's Expanded Exhaustive Concordance of the Bible* (Nashville: Thomas Nelson, 2009), s.v. "tetelestai"

[6] John 19:28

[7] Psalm 8:1-9

[8] Genesis 2:2

[9] Matthew 7:14

[10] Exodus 40:33

[11] Hebrews 4:16

[12] Philippians 3:20

[13] Warren W. Wiersbe, *The Cross of Jesus: What His Words from Calvary Mean for Us*. (Grand Rapids, MI: Baker Publishing, 1997). Kindle Edition. Loc 1198-1240.

[14] Leviticus 1:3

[15] John 1:36

[16] Hebrews 10:14

[17] Ephesians 1:7

[18] Steven Furtick, *Seven-Mile Miracle: Experience the Last Words of Christ As Never Before*. (Colorado Springs, CO: Multnomah Press, 2017). Chapter 6.

[19] Luke 2:35

[20] Luke 22:42

[21] Mark 7:36

[22] John 4:34

[23] John 6:38

[24] Romans 5:14

[25] Genesis 3:15

[26] Genesis 22:13

[27] Psalm 19:7-10

[28] Psalm 1:3

[29] Matthew 5:17

[30] C.S. Lewis, *Mere Christianity* (New York: HarperOne, 2017), p 52.

[31] Erwin W. Lutzer, *Cries from the Cross: A Journey into the Heart of Jesus* (Chicago: Moody Publishers, 2015), Kindle Edition. 112.

[32] Galatians 2:20

Step Seven - Rest in God

"Father, into your hands I commit my spirit."
Luke 23:46

During a basketball game in middle school gym class, I went up for a rebound and broke my finger. As I was jumping to get the ball, it came down and hit my finger at a terrible angle. The fingernail was split and, as the doctor would later explain, the bone just above the knuckle was fractured. Ouch.

Thankfully, this was not a serious injury. But it would require a minor surgery that evening. It was a routine operation, and they had me out in a couple of hours. They gave me some pain medications, signed my cast, and sent me on my way. I was flying pretty high.

That night, I woke up in terrible pain. The medicine wore off. The tip of my finger felt like it was on fire, and pain was pulsing through my body. I began to cry. Then I began to wail. Everything hurt.

Looking back, I wonder if the pain was actually that intense or if I was just scared. At twelve years old, I had never experienced that sort of physical pain. I liked to rough house and had my fair share of bruises. An older brother kept a steady measure of charley horses on my biceps. But this was different. Pain was coursing through my body, and I did not know when, or if, it would stop.

In the midst of my crying, I remember hearing my mother's footsteps. She opened the door and a cascade of light poured onto the bed where I lay crying. She sat down on the bed and put her arms around my neck. Mom put her cheek next to mine and began to whisper in my ear. In a language that only loving mothers know, she spoke words of comfort.

The pain began to subside. I stopped trembling. The tears on my face began to dry. My finger still hurt, but I was not scared anymore. I could rest.

I do not remember what she said. I wish I could. But the words were not as important as her presence. If I had written down what she said for posterity's sake, the words likely would not mean much on paper. It was not her words that calmed me; it was her presence. Her company relived my fear.

Step Seven - Rest in God

At the seventh and final word from the cross, we witness Jesus finding rest in the comfort of his Father. His body was subjected to terrible cruelty. He cried out in the pain of separation ("My God, my God, why have you forsaken me?") and in physical anguish ("I thirst"). But at the last, his words were an expression of the rest he had in God.

This final word from the cross brings us to *Step Seven: Rest in God*. The aim of the believer is to enjoy divine rest in God. As we have seen, each word from the cross represents a new stage of spiritual growth. Some of these stages are exciting, like *Step Two: New Citizenship*, when we embrace the promises of God, and *Step Three: A New Community*, when we join the church. Other stages are tumultuous. We wrestle with God, and our hearts begin to thirst for true justice. Each of these steps is moving us toward the goal: *Step Seven: Rest in God*.

God designed humanity to enjoy life with him. At creation, we see God's desire was constant, unending communion. In the Garden of Eden, God walked and talked freely with his children. Adam and Eve would work, but it was not burdensome. They were at peace with God, living in his rest. Again, this does not mean they were lying around all day in the garden! Eden was a busy place. But they had satisfaction in their relationship with God.

Sin destroyed the harmony of Eden. The relationship Adam and Eve enjoyed with God was broken. Work became laborious. They began to argue with him and with one another. Sin created restlessness.

Much of life is a search for rest. We want Divine peace. Our hearts ache for contentment. We want to be satisfied. The effects of sin mean we lack balance. Our lives are out of order. We work too much or not enough. We have trouble finding a good rhythm of life. We can engage in all sorts of leisure activities and travel to any number of vacation destinations. We may relax our bodies, but our spirits remain restless.

As a pastor, I have been privileged to meet some of the finest saints in the kingdom. There are a precious few who find lasting rest in their lives with God. They are content. The peace of God emanates from their words and actions. They reflect Christ within. And these folks do not sit still! Do not imagine these peaceful souls sitting sedentary waiting for eternity! They are in the Word every day. They are prayer warriors. These saints are active in the kingdom: teaching, serving, mentoring, and, if necessary, admonishing their brothers and sisters in Christ. But through it all, there is peace. Rest. Solace. Their hearts are at ease because they have found rest in him.

There is no measuring rod for peace with God. There is no box to check. In my experience, those who come to a place of rest in God are those who have been through the mire. They have had pain and grief in life; some continue to endure suffering. Yet they walk in the calm assurance of God's plan.

A story is told of an elderly Christian, a dear saint of God. One day, he was tending his garden, and a young man asked him what he would do if he knew that Christ would return tomorrow. The elder Christian gently replied, "I would continue to plant my garden." He knew that, at that moment, he was supposed to be tending his garden. It was God's work for him on that day. Those who rest in God have the calm assurance of his work in the world. At his last breath, Jesus confidently expressed his rest in God.

Into Your Hands, I Commit My Spirit.

The seventh word is a final note in God's ensemble of salvation. Jesus offered his entire self, body and soul, to the hands of God. This was not a cry of desperation or abandonment. Jesus was certain he was returning to the presence of God. The last words uttered from the cross are from Psalm 31:5. This was a household prayer, as common as "Now I lay me down to sleep" or "God is great, God is good, thank you Lord, for this food." Little boys and girls were taught to repeat this line, usually before bedtime:

> *Into your hand I commit my spirit; you have redeemed me, O Lord, faithful God.*[1](ESV)

In death, as in life, Jesus was meditating on Scripture. Jesus is the Word. He is the fulfillment of the Scriptures. At the end of his earthly life, Jesus was leaning on the words that encompassed his ministry. Instead of a weighty theological diatribe, Jesus repeated the prayer of a child.

A careful look reveals that Jesus did not say the whole line. Jesus omitted the second line in the verse, which acknowledges

God's redemption (padah/פָּדָה).[2] Jesus did not need redemption; he is the redeemer. He was without sin and perfect in obedience to God. His only desire was to rest in God.

These moments before Jesus "gave up his spirit"[3] were relief to the suffering Savior. He endured six hours on the cross. From the cross, he first addressed those nearby: his enemies, convicts, and family. He cried to God in separation, spoke of his physical longings, and told the world that salvation was "finished." Now, at the last, Jesus spoke to God with the innocence of a child. He was returning to the Father.

The last recorded word from the cross is an echo of Jesus's first recorded words: "Don't you know I have to be about my Father's business?"[4] On Calvary, Jesus was finishing the work his Father sent him to do. Jesus was entering his Father's rest.

Jesus's words in death are an expression of his life. People die in the same way they live. If hatred is allowed to dwell in the heart in life, it will likely remain in death. Some believe they can live however they like, in malice and sin, and just repent in the final moments. But people do not know when their final moments will come. If people put off the gospel in the comfort of life, they will likely reject Jesus in the dreariness of death.

Voltaire was a prolific writer, historian, and philosopher in the seventeenth century; he was also an avowed atheist. He used his gift of prose to attack the Christian faith. He said of Jesus, "Curse the wretch. In twenty years, Christianity will be no more. My single hand will destroy the edifice it took twelve apostles to rear." (Spoiler alert: Voltaire was not successful.) His final days were agonizing. He was miserable as he neared death, cursing that his time was so short. One of his nurses remarked, "For all of the wealth in Europe, I would not watch another atheist die." According to his physician, who was nearby at Voltaire's death, the famed author said, "I am abandoned by God and man. I will give half of what I am worth if you will give me six months of life. Then I will go to hell and you will go with me, oh Christ, oh Jesus Christ."[5] Voltaire died as he lived. But Jesus trusted God in life and, in death, his last words were spoken in the calm assurance of his faithfulness. At the last word from the cross, we see a Savior who was dying just as he lived.

At our church, we had a dear brother in Christ who suffered from severe dementia. His elderly body was relatively strong, but his mind was weak. He could not remember one moment to the next. But when his family would gather around to sing hymns and read Scripture, he would mouth the words to the gospel songs. He would close his eyes and fold his hands to pray, even though he could not comprehend the words of the prayer.

In his final days, this dear brother in Christ had a moment of clarity. He smiled at his daughter and said, "Jesus is real!" Every other memory had slipped away. His body had become frail. The years of sickness had stripped away every last ounce of strength. The only thing left was his great love for Jesus. The gospel was in his bones. This man died as he lived: in loving relationship with God. His last thoughts were of his first love.

"Into your hands": Why did Jesus commit himself to the "hands" of God? It would seem that he might commit to the heart of God, which would reflect intimacy with the Father. Jesus did not say anything about the face of God, which represents the glory of the Father. Jesus shares equally in God's majesty, so he does not mention his face. Of course, Jesus would not commit himself to the feet of God, as he is not subservient to him.

In his last moments, Jesus said he was committing himself to God's hands. You can tell a lot about people by their hands. As a boy, I remember feeling the calluses on my grandfather's palms. He was a long-time pastor but spent his (limited) free time as a cattle farmer. The hardened wells of skin told the story of a man who both cared for souls and wrangled the cows. Throughout Scripture, God's interaction with his people is often referred to as his hands. Depending on the context, God's hands can be gentle or firm. They are for care and judgment.

Similarly, the hands of Jesus were both gentle and firm. In the Old Testament, God used his mighty hand to care for and judge the people of Israel. In the New, Jesus used his in similar ways, revealing the compassion and justice of God. As seen in Scripture, the hands of God are a place of:

Priority: The right hand of God is a place of priority. It is reserved as the highest seat of honor and for a representative of the king. The disciples argued with one another about who would get to be seated at Jesus's right hand. Stephen had a vision of Jesus, seated at the right hand of God. The Apostles' Creed affirms the scriptural witness: "He ascended into heaven and sits at the right hand of God the Father almighty."

Only Jesus is worthy to sit at the right hand of God. As Philippians 2 tells us, Jesus "was in very nature God."[6] Giving up his position in glory, Jesus came to earth to enter our human condition, suffer our temptation, bear our sin, and die on Calvary. He "made himself nothing by taking the very nature of a servant" and would "become obedient to death—even death on a cross!"[7]

By committing himself to the hands of God, Jesus was returning to his rightful place. At his death, as the spirit was given up, Jesus was "exalted…to the highest place and [given] the name that is above every name."[8]

Rebuilding: The history of Israel is a story of conflict. Their great city, Jerusalem, has been destroyed and rebuilt numerous times. As the Hebrews were returning to Jerusalem under Persian King Artaxerxes, Nehemiah asked if he could return and rebuild the city walls, which were in ruins. The request should have been a non-starter, as Nehemiah was a high servant of the king. But God's hand was over the situation. Nehemiah was allowed to return, and the king even supplied the building material! Nehemiah would write: "Because the gracious hand of my God was on me, the king granted my requests."[9] With God's helping hand, Nehemiah was able to rebuild the walls around Jerusalem, thereby securing a safe return to their capital city.

However, it was Jesus who had the greatest rebuilding project! Jesus said, "Destroy this temple, and I will raise it again in three days."[10] Everyone assumed he was talking about the greatest structure in Israel's history, Solomon's Temple. It was a massive house of worship that took years to construct. How could Jesus ever tear down and rebuild something so massive? But Jesus was not referring to the man-made Temple. He was speaking of his body. He is the Temple of God. People were once commanded to worship God in an exact location by perpetually offering sacrifices. But now Jesus is the perfect sacrifice, and worship can happen wherever he is present. His body, the temple of worship, would be destroyed on Calvary, but by the hand of God, it would be rebuilt in three days. Jesus was committing himself to the hands of God, who would rebuild his body just as the walls of Jerusalem generations before.

Resurrection: In the days of the prophet Ezekiel, things looked bleak for God's people. They were defeated, exiled, and spiritually destitute. From the wilderness, the prophet cried out in desperation. He longed for Israel to be physically and spiritually restored.

Ezekiel recorded that the "hand of the Lord was on me,"[11] and he was taken to the middle of a destitute valley full of dead men's bones. These remains represent the spiritual and physical death of God's people as they had been subject to defeat by their enemies. Ezekiel was led "back and forth among them and [he] saw many bones on the floor of the valley, bones that were very dry."[12] The prophet asked, "Can these dry bones live?"[13]

Ezekiel, with the hand of the Lord upon him, was told to "prophesy to these bones and say to them, 'dry bones, hear the word of the Lord!'" He goes on:

> *This is what the Sovereign Lord says to these bones: I will make breath enter you, and you will come to life. I will attach tendons to you and make flesh come upon you and cover you with skin; I will put breath in you, and you will come to life. Then you will know that I am the Lord!*[14]

As the prophet spoke the word of the Lord, the bones began to rattle together and flesh formed around them. They stood and received new breath and life! They gathered together and were "an exceedingly great army."[15]

At the cross, Jesus was suffering the worst fate. Instead of dry bones in a valley, he was sagging, exhausted flesh on the cross. But he committed himself to the hand of God, who can make the dead live again. We are born into iniquity, and our souls are dead in sin. We are the lifeless, dry bones of a war-torn valley. When Jesus died on the cross, he committed himself to a God who can make dry bones live. When we receive him, we join him in his death and resurrection:

> *For we believe that Jesus died and rose again, and so we believe that God will bring with Jesus those who have fallen asleep in him.*[16]

Liberation: The Hebrew people suffered under Egyptian bondage for generations. They cried out to God for help, and he provided rescue. Exodus tells us that God saved his people with his hand:

> *Now you will see what I will do to Pharaoh: Because of my mighty hand he will let them go; because of my mighty hand he will drive them out of his country!*[17]

God rescued his people by the power of his hand!

Jesus suffered terrible bondage on Calvary. Theologically speaking, Jesus was "alienated," which refers to an absolute inability for self-governance. He was enslaved by the cross. But Jesus committed himself to God, who liberates his people with his mighty hand. By committing to his Father's hands, Jesus was certain of his impending freedom. The cross could not hold Jesus because God was on his side. The gospel message is always a message of liberation. Jesus sets the captives free. In his inaugural message, Jesus said he had come to liberate the poor and to set the captives free. Those who commit themselves to Christ are living in the promises of God, who uses his hand to rescue the spiritually and physically oppressed.

Care: One of the first songs I learned as a small child was "He's got the whole world, in his hands!" With joy and confidence, we sing about a God who holds everything with tender care. God is caring and gracious. This is why Jesus taught us to refer to him in prayer as "Father." He cares for us like a parent cares for his children. Like a parent, God forms us into something better than we could be on our own. The prophet Jeremiah refers to God's formative work as "potter's hands":

> *Like clay in the hand of the potter, so are you in my hand, Israel.*[18]

Though his body had been beaten and torn, Jesus was not formed by the hands of his enemies. It was God who had the final say in his masterpiece. Jesus committed himself to the hands of a Father who would pull his broken body from the grave and restore what the world had broken. This is good news for the faithful, too.

We may suffer at the hands of our accusers and feel the indignities of this world. But God's hands are continually forming us into his image. Though struggles may come our way, we can hold the hand of God:

> *For I am the Lord your God who takes hold of your right hand and says to you, Do not fear; I will help you.*[19]

Jesus used his hands to care and heal. Though he could heal from a distance, Jesus often went through the act of putting his hands on the afflicted. He spit into dirt and rubbed the mud on the face of a blind man.[20] When a leper came to him for healing, Jesus ignored the usual procedure (run away!) and put his hands on the man's head.[21] In one of the more tender moments of the gospels, Jesus took the hand of a young girl who had died and brought her back to life.[22] He literally felt the pain of the sick and vulnerable. On the cross, those hands were pierced by people who were threatened by his gentle healing touch.

A large crowd followed Jesus into the wilderness to hear his teaching. He preached all morning, and people were getting hungry for lunch. The disciples told Jesus to send the crowds away to nearby towns so they could eat. But Jesus told the disciples, "You feed them."[23] At this, Jesus took the bread in his hands, blessed it, and multiplied the food into enough to feed thousands.

In another act of incredible service, Jesus washed the feet of the disciples.[24] On the night before he was arrested, he stooped to their feet, wearing only a towel, and performed the job of a servant. This was a foreshadowing of the next night, when Jesus, again wearing only a loincloth, would perform the greatest act of service. The disciples that Jesus was serving would go on to either abandon or betray him. He knew this, and yet he served them with his own hands.

Judgment: Of course, the hands of God are not all about tender care. The hand of God is stern. Throughout Scripture, God judged with precision and severity. Though the unrighteous may thrive for a time, their day is coming. The author of Hebrews reminds us:

> *It is a dreadful thing to fall into the hands of
> the living God.*[25]

Those who oppress the poor and prey on the vulnerable will know the judgment of God. Those who reject him will feel the wrath of his hands. In eternity, we will know God's hands: either as a gentle touch or firm punishment.

The judgment of God is perfect. In the parable of the persistent widow, a woman came before a judge and begged for justice.[26] She refused to be dismissed before her case was heard. Those who are righteous do not fear the justice of God. The psalmist cries out for justice:

> *Judge me, O Lord, according to my
> righteousness and according to the integrity
> that is in me.*[27]

Jesus committed himself to the hand of God and his righteous justice. He had nothing to fear. He did not dread the hand of God, but welcomed his touch. Those who rest in Christ have the same assurance.

Jesus used his hands for the cause of justice. Enraged at the money changing and exploitation of the poor, Jesus made a whip and cleared the Temple.[28] It had become common practice to sell animal sacrifices at a higher rate in the Temple complex. People who could not afford to bring sacrifices with them had to pay more in Jerusalem. The wealthy were taking advantage of the spiritual obligations of the poor. He was furious that the vulnerable were being exploited and in God's house, no less. The gentle peasant from Galilee became zealous for justice in the house of God.

Handiwork: Creation is a masterpiece. He has crafted his creation with innumerable colors and textures. The night sky is a canvas on which God painted billions of stars. Our God is not a bland bureaucrat. He is an artist. The psalmist refers to creation as "God's handiwork."[29] God formed the masterpiece of creation with his hand. In the creation account, we read that God declared each separate part of the world "good." Humans were deemed "very good."[30] God's greatest work is in creating humanity, which was crafted in his image. But sin has shattered his artwork. Sinful humanity does not live up to the beauty for which we were created. Disobedience and distance mark our existence.

Jesus is the masterpiece of God's intention. He is everything that humanity was supposed to be. God intended that we would offer him glory and live in obedience. Though we have failed, Jesus came as the perfect emblem of humanity. He was perfect in obedience and always glorified God!

Of course, Jesus did not look like a work of art from the cross. He was bloodied, beaten, and, by every measure, defeated. But God had not completed the final stroke of this portrait. By committing himself to the hands of God, Jesus knew that the story was not over. The same God who took the formless, chaotic void and turned it into a majestic creation would restore the bloody mess of the cross and make it beautiful.

The hands that served and fed were nailed to the cross. He was no longer able to reach, touch, and heal. His hands bound, and his arms held wide, Jesus committed himself to the hands of his Father, expecting his embrace.

"I commit my Spirit": Jesus entrusted his spirit to the hands of the Father. The gospel writers did not find it sufficient to say, "He died." Rather, they remarked that Jesus "gave up his spirit."[31] This death was more than the absence of a heartbeat. Jesus offered his spirit to God and relinquished it at the foreordained time.

To better understand the gravity of the moment, we should pause here to consider the juxtaposition of flesh and spirit. The terms that attempt to define the spiritual nature of humanity are somewhat ambiguous. We use terms like "spirit," "soul," and "heart" interchangeably. But Jesus used a term that requires our attention.

Specifically, Jesus committed his "spirit" to God. Spirit comes from the Greek word pneuma (πνεῦμα)[32] and also means wind or breath. Most of the uses in Scripture for pneuma are in reference to the Holy Spirit. But Jesus spoke of his spirit. In this sense, the spirit is the "dimension of human personality whereby relationship with God is possible. It is this spiritual nature that enables continuing conversation with the divine Spirit."[33] Every person has a spirit. The spirit encompasses our being. It is the unseen, inert spiritual self that makes possible our communion with God. True worship, that is acceptable to God, is from our spirit and not our flesh.[34] We are more than flesh and blood. We have spiritual bodies.

The spiritual body is contrasted with the flesh, which is ever forming, growing, changing, aging, and (inevitably) dying. The temporal flesh is unalterably opposed to the inward spirit.[35] Both body and spirit are corruptible, but it is flesh that is easier prey for sin.

On Calvary, Jesus offered his body, every fiber of flesh, to God in sacrifice. He endured the torture of crucifixion and shed blood as atonement for sin. His body, unlike ours, never succumbed to sin. Though tempted by the devil himself, Jesus never indulged the flesh. His body was offered to God in perfect submission.

Now, at the last, Jesus committed the spirit. This was all he had left to offer. The fullness of the Son was offered to the Father. This is, as the hymn proclaims, "perfect submission, perfect delight."[36] His sinless body and eternal spirit were at rest. While our flesh wages war with our spirit, Jesus offered both in harmony to God.

Enter into His Rest

Here then is the vision of true and divine rest. Jesus has completed the work in both body and soul. He was at rest with God. The saving work of God in Christ was done. All of the desires of God have been fulfilled in Christ. Jesus is forever the "yes" of God's promises.[37]

Because of the death of Jesus, God's people can finally reach the rest he promised long before. Following Joshua, God's people were en route to the promised land. But in the desolate wilderness they became hard-hearted. At Meribah, they were disobedient to God's commands. God declared his anger:

> *For forty years I was angry with that generation; I said, 'They are a people whose hearts go astray, and they have not known my ways.' So I declared on oath in my anger, 'They shall never enter my rest.'*[38]

Under Moses, and Joshua after him, the people of God were not given rest. Their disobedience led to punishment and unrest. But Jesus is the completion of the work God began centuries before. Jesus is the new Moses, the fulfillment of the Law. He is the new Joshua, mighty victor over the greatest opponents: sin and death. Jesus leads his followers to the new promised land. This is not an earthly nation, but an eternal home for the faithful:

> *I go and prepare a place for you, I will come back and take you to be with me that you also may be where I am.*[39]

Revelation speaks of the rest believers enjoy in eternity:

> *'Never again will they hunger; never again will they thirst. The sun will not beat down on them,' nor any scorching heat. For the Lamb at the center of the throne will be their shepherd; 'he will lead them to springs of living water.' 'And God will wipe away every tear from their eyes.'*[40]

In heaven, the eternity promised to the Good Thief and everyone who calls on his name, Jesus promises a rest from labor.

This rest is not only a promise for the afterlife. We can taste the heavenly shalom even now. Jesus offers peace to the restless heart: "Come to me, all you who are weary and burdened, and I will give you rest."[41] The aim of the spiritual life is not intellect or influence. We do not gauge our spiritual maturity by the number of miracles we perform or masses we attract. A life with God is not defined by what we do for him. Rather, the marker of a deep life with God is how we rest in him.

The cross reminds us that God does not promise a calm journey, only a safe landing. The last glimpses of Jesus were of a bloodied, defeated peasant who whispered a child's prayer before his death. But this morbid scene was the culmination of a grand and glorious plan, one that ensures eternal peace for those who believe. His death and the offering of his spirit ensured that we too can find rest for our wandering hearts.

Step Seven - Rest in God

[1] Psalm 31:5

[2] James Strong, *Strong's Expanded Exhaustive Concordance of the Bible* (Nashville: Thomas Nelson, 2009), s.v. "padah"

[3] Matthew 27:50, Mark 15:37, Luke 23:46, John 19:30

[4] Luke 2:49

[5] Greg Laurie. *Finding Hope in the Last Words of Jesus*. (Grand Rapids: Baker Publishing Group, 2009) Kindle Edition, 8-9.

[6] Philippians 2:6

[7] Philippians 2:8

[8] Philippians 2:9

[9] Nehemiah 2:8

[10] John 2:19

[11] Ezekiel 37:1

[12] Ezekiel 37:2

[13] Ezekiel 37:3

[14] Ezekiel 37:5-6

[15] Ezekiel 37:10

[16] 1 Thessalonians 4:14

[17] Exodus 6:1

[18] Jeremiah 18:6

[19] Isaiah 41:13

[20] John 9:1-12

[21] Matthew 8:1-4, Mark 1:40-45 and Luke 5:12-16

[22] Luke 8:40-53

[23] Mark 6:37

[24] John 13:1-17

[25] Hebrews 10:31

[26] Luke 18:1-8

[27] Psalm 7:8

[28] John 2:13-22

[29] Psalm 19:1

[30] Genesis 1:31

[31] Matthew 27:50, Mark 15:37, Luke 23:46, John 19:30

[32] James Strong, *Strong's Expanded Exhaustive Concordance of the Bible* (Nashville: Thomas Nelson, 2009), s.v. "pneuma"

[33] Walter A. Elwell ed. *Baker Theological Dictionary of the Bible*. Grand Rapids, MI: Baker Books, 1996. "spirit"

[34] John 4:24

[35] Galatians 5:16-17

[36] Fanny Crosby. Hymn: Blessed Assurance

[37] 2 Corinthians 1:20

[38] Psalm 95:10-11

[39] John 14:3

[40] Revelation 7:16-17

[41] Matthew 11:28

Epilogue

I have learned more from he crucifix than from any book.
Thomas Aquinas

Jesus led three disciples to the top of a mountain where he revealed a glimpse of his divine nature. On the mountain of transfiguration, Jesus meta-morphed (μεταμορφόω/metamorphoó) and "his face shone like the sun, and his clothes became as white as the light" (Matthew 17:2). The disciples, amazed and befuddled, were witness to the glory of God in flesh, Jesus Christ. The trip up the mountain was a difficult task. No doubt their legs were tired and cramped from the climb. They probably mumbled under their breath as they trudged along. But the trek was worth the hassle. Jesus called them to a difficult journey, but a majestic moment waited at the end.

Calvary too is a mountain, but one that only Jesus could climb. His followers could get a glimpse of his glory at the Mount of Transfiguration, but they could not know his pain at Mount Calvary. On the cross, Jesus bore the sin and death that we deserved. By his shed blood our sins are forgiven and we can commune with God. This is a work that only Jesus could accomplish.

Even though Jesus had to make this journey alone, he continued to reveal the way to the father. Battered, bleeding and bruised, Jesus still thought of his followers and called them closer to God.

The Seven Last Words invite us to a full life with God. Many believers just want the Transfiguration moment; give us the glory of worship and the thrill of his presence! But there is more to a life with God. To follow Jesus means we give our whole life to following in his footsteps. This means there will be joy and sorrow, tragedy and celebration, exasperation and rest. The seven last words from the cross represent the whole journey with Jesus, through good times and bad.

God is calling you to take the next step. Wherever you are in your walk with Jesus, there is always another step to take. We never really "arrive" in our journey with God; at least not on this side of heaven.

So take a moment to consider your journey with Jesus.

Epilogue

Where are you?

> Step One - **Receiving Forgiveness.** "Father, forgive them, for they do not know what they are doing" (Luke 23:34).
>
> Step Two - **New Citizenship.** "Truly I tell you, today you will be with me in Paradise" (Luke 23:43).
>
> Step Three - **A New Community.** "Woman, here is your son. Here is your mother" (John 19:26–27).
>
> Step Four- **Wrestling with God.** "My God, my God, why have you forsaken me?" (Mark 15:34; Matthew 27:46).
>
> Step Five - **New Thirst.** "I am thirsty" (John 19:28).
>
> Step Six - **Confidence in Salvation.** "It is finished" (John 19:30).
>
> Step Seven -**Rest in God.** "Father, into your hands I commit my spirit" (Luke 23:46).

Are you enjoying the forgiveness of God? Great! Move to strengthen your citizenship in the kingdom of heaven. Are you engaged in the life of the church, but not growing spiritually? Lean into the deeper mysterious of a God who is sometimes silent but always faithful. Transform your desires into his desires and thirst for the things of God. But do not stop at inward transformation! Go deeper. Take the next step! Have full confidence in the salvation won on Calvary; it is finished! Each step leads us to our hearts desire - rest in God.

Wherever you are, don't stop climbing. Take the next step. God is calling you to his rest. Jesus ascended on Mount Calvary to win our salvation and with his final words, he extended an invitation. Will you listen to the words from this mountain? Will you heed the call to a deeper life with God? Will you take the next step?

> ***The Lord makes firm the steps of the one who delights in him; though he may stumble, he will not fall, for the Lord upholds him with his hand. (Psalm 37:23-24)***

Bibliography

Brueggemann, Walter. *Into Your Hand: Confronting Good Friday.* Eugene, OR: Cascade Books, 2014.

Elwell, Walter A. ed. *Baker Theological Dictionary of the Bible.* Grand Rapids, MI: Baker Books, 1996.

Fox, George. *The Journal of George Fox.* Rufas Jones, ed. Richmond, IN: Friends United Press, 1997.

Furtick, Steven. *Seven-Mile Miracle: Experience the Last Words of Christ As Never Before.* Colorado Springs, CO: Multnomah Press, 2017.

Haurwas, Stanley. The Cross-Shattered Christ: Mediations on the Seven Last Words. Ada, MI: Brazos Press, 2005.

Laurie, Greg. *Finding Hope in the Last Words of Jesus.* Grand Rapids, MI: Baker Publishing Group, 2009.

Lewis, C.S. Mere Christianity. New York: Harper Collins Publishing, 2017.

Lutzer, Erwin W. *Cries from the Cross: A Journey into the Heart of Jesus.* Chicago: Moody Publishers, 2015.

Martin, James. *Seven Last Words: An Invitation to a Deeper Friendship with Jesus.* New York: HarperOne, 2015.

Teresa, E. Allison Peers, and Teresa. 1988. *Interior castle.* New York, N.Y.: Doubleday.

Pink, Arthur W. *The Seven Sayings of the Saviour on the Cross.* Arthur Pink Collection Book 49. Prisbrary Publishing.

Rutledge, Fleming. *The Seven Last Words from the Cross.* Grand Rapids, MI: Eerdmans, 2005.

Sheen, Fulton J. *The Cries of Jesus From the Cross: A Fulton Sheen Anthology*. Manchester, NH: Sophia Institute Press, 2018.

———. *Life of Christ*. New York: Double Day Publishing, 1990.

Spurgeon, C. H. *Christ's Words from the Cross*. Titus Books. Kindle Edition. Titus Books, 2014.

Stott, John. *The Cross of Christ*. Downers Grove, IL: IVP Books, 2006.

Strong, James. *Strong's Expanded Exhaustive Concordance of the Bible*. Nashville: Thomas Nelson, 2009.

The Holy Bible, New International Version. Grand Rapids: Zondervan Publishing House, 1984.

Wiersbe, Warren W. *The Cross of Jesus: What His Words from Calvary Mean for Us*. Grand Rapids, MI: Baker Publishing Group, 1997.

Willimon, William. *Thank God It's Friday: Encountering the Seven Last Words from the Cross*. Nashville: Abingdon Press, 2006.

Vita

David Mercadante serves as Senior Pastor of Poplar Ridge Friends Meeting in Trinity, North Carolina. He holds a B.A. in Religion from High Point University, a Master of Divinity from Wake Forest University and a Doctor of Ministry from Gordon-Conwell Theological Seminary. David has served in ministry since 1998, mostly in Friends (Quaker) ministries. In 2006, David married Emily and they have four beautiful children together: Lucy, Maggie, Oliver and Hope.

Made in the USA
Coppell, TX
29 January 2021

49097748R00080